**Philadelphia Behavioral Health Services Transformation**

**Practice Guidelines for Recovery and Resilience Oriented Treatment**

**Transformation is more jazz
than scored music.**

William L. White

Version 1.1
First published in
The United States of America
AuthorHouse™ LLC
1663 Liberty Drive
Bloomington, IN 47403
www.authorhouse.com
Phone: 1-800-839-8640
ISBN: 978-1-4918-2890-8 (sc)
ISBN: 978-1-4918-2889-2 (hc)
ISBN: 978-1-4918-2888-5 (e)
Library of Congress
Control Number: 2013918965
Layout design: Sadé Ali
Cover design: Monava Jones

Printed in the USA on acid free paper

PHILADELPHIA BEHAVIORAL HEALTH SERVICES
# TRANSFORMATION

# PRACTICE GUIDELINES
## FOR RECOVERY AND RESILIENCE ORIENTED TREATMENT

Co-Authors
Ijeoma Achara Abrahams, PsyD
OmiSadé Ali, MA
Larry Davidson, PhD
Arthur C. Evans, PhD
Joan Kenerson King, RN, MSN, APRN-BC
Paul Poplawski, PhD
William L. White, MA

Philadelphia Department of Behavioral Health
and Intellectual disAbility Services

City of Philadelphia

DBHIDS

DEPARTMENT of BEHAVIORAL HEALTH
and INTELLECTUAL disABILITY SERVICES

Recovery, Resilience & Self-Determination

# Letter from
## Arthur C. Evans, Jr., PhD

Dear Stakeholders,

We are at a critical juncture in the history of healthcare in the United States. The recently enacted healthcare reform legislation is shifting the landscape for all health-related services. Philadelphia is extremely fortunate to be building on a long history of innovative services, and so we are poised to meet the challenges of this new era in healthcare.

These *Practice Guidelines for Resilience-and Recovery-oriented Treatment* represent the next phase in the evolution of Philadelphia's behavioral health system. They are based on the collective work and ideas of many stakeholders throughout the system. The guidelines are rooted in the voices of people in recovery and their family members, as well as treatment providers, advocates and system administrators, who together have developed a shared vision for our behavioral health system. Your feedback has been blended with the lessons learned from Philadelphia's transformation efforts over the past 30 years, several exciting national trends and the empirically informed practices documented in the literature. Together these form the foundation for Philadelphia's new practice guidelines.

This document is the first of three that are designed to guide our system in delivering services and supports that promote recovery and resilience. However, fully integrating these practices into the system—and into people's lives— will require significant changes in the fiscal, policy, regulatory and community contexts. To address these needs, the second document in this series will focus on the changes that are necessary in the overall system to support the implementation of these practices. These will include changes in fiscal, policy, performance improvement, credentialing and evaluation strategies. The third and final document in this series will explore the role of the broader community in promoting recovery and resilience. That document will be written in the context of the emerging federal direction around the critical role of the community in prevention, early intervention and the promotion of overall health.

I would like to thank you for your tireless efforts and unwavering commitment to improving the lives of people with behavioral health challenges in the City of Philadelphia. It is my hope that the guidelines contained in this document will serve as a catalyst for ongoing innovation and dialogue as we work together to make our system even stronger.

Sincerely,
Arthur C. Evans, Jr., PhD, Commissioner
Department of Behavioral Health
and Intellectual disAbility Services

# Acknowledgments

# Transformation of Behavioral Health Services in Philadelphia

## Co-authors

Ijeoma Achara Abrahams, PsyD
OmiSadé Ali, MA
Larry Davidson, PhD
Arthur C. Evans, PhD
Joan Kenerson King, RN, MSN, APRN-BC
Paul Poplawski, PhD
William L. White, MA

## Contributors (Focus Group Participants/Reviewers)

Altarum Institute, Washington, DC
Compact Family Member Committee
Consumer Satisfaction Team
Consumer & Family Task Force
DBHIDS Staff
Faith Based initiative
Family Resource Network
LGBTQ Initiative
Mental Health Association of Southeastern PA
Office of Addiction Services Advisory Board
Recovery Advisory Committee
Parents Involved Network
Person First Taskforce
Philadelphia Alliance
Philadelphia Coalition
Philadelphia Compact for Children's Services
Philadelphia Peer Leadership Academy
Philadelphia Psychiatric Society
PROACT
Youth MOVE Philadelphia

Over the past eight years, many individuals, providers and stakeholders participated in focus groups and review processes to assist in the development and refinement of the practice guidelines. It has been the innovative and transforming work of the Philadelphia Behavioral Health System stakeholders that has informed and inspired the development of the practice guidelines.

# CONTENTS

# Section I: Introduction

## History

## Momentum from National Trends

# Section I: Introduction

# History

Philadelphia has had a long history of innovation in the behavioral health field, beginning with the work of Dr. Benjamin Rush (1746-1813), the first to propose a disease concept of "chronic drunkenness" and to advocate specialized treatment services for this condition. The city's leadership role continued with the closing of the state hospitals in the late 1980s and the more recent formation of Community Behavioral Health (CBH), the nation's largest city-controlled managed behavioral healthcare organization. This document represents the next step in the evolution of Philadelphia's efforts to create a more effective and efficient system of care. This system is based on the latest thinking in the field, empirical evidence and another essential element: the preferences of the individuals and families receiving services.

These practice guidelines are framed by the notions of recovery and resilience. It is this framework, and an unwavering belief in recovery and resilience in behavioral health, that should be the basis for service delivery. The document is presented in three sections:

I.   Introduction

II.  Overview of the Framework

III. Strategies in the Four Domains

The guidelines presented in this report represent the collective vision of many people. Hundreds of stakeholders—including people in recovery, providers, family members, advocates and staff of the Philadelphia Department of Behavioral Health and Intellectual disAbility Services (DBHIDS)[1]—participated in focus groups across the behavioral health system, contributing their ideas and perspectives about existing strengths, best and promising practices and opportunities for growth.

Their feedback has been blended with the lessons learned from Philadelphia's transformation efforts over the past 30 years, several exciting national trends and the empirically informed practices documented in the literature. Together they form the foundation for Philadelphia's new practice guidelines.

---

[1] Until March 1, 2011, this agency was called the Department of Behavioral Health and Mental Retardation Services (DBH/MRS). For clarity and simplicity, it will be referred to with its new name, and new acronym, throughout this document.

## Section I: Introduction

# Momentum from National Trends

Several national trends are propelling the dramatic changes unfolding within the City of Philadelphia's behavioral health system. These trends include national health care reform efforts, mental health transformation processes, the recovery advocacy movement in the addiction field, the emphasis on resilience in children's behavioral health and findings published in the Institute of Medicine's *Quality Chasm* report.

## Health Care Reform: Quality, Outcomes and Accountability

The historic health care reform legislation enacted on March 23, 2010 holds the potential to transform the landscape on which all healthcare services are delivered. In addition to extending health care coverage to an estimated 32 million more Americans, health care reform promises to improve the quality of care and increase the focus on outcomes and accountability.

Some of the implications of health care reform for behavioral health include:

- an increased focus on the coordination between and integration of specialty behavioral health services and primary care;
- a greater focus on comprehensive, "whole health" approaches that address the full range of needs of individuals receiving services;
- increased focus on supporting people in lower levels of care (e.g., services in community-based settings) rather than higher, more restrictive services (e.g., residential, inpatient, partial hospitalization programs);
- greater attention to treatment outcomes and provider accountability; and
- a focus on measures that will enhance the infrastructure (service systems and providers) to support the delivery of effective services (e.g., greater utilization of health information technology).

## Mental Health Transformation: A Place in the Community

These substantive reforms in behavioral health policy and practice are not occurring in a vacuum. In recent years, behavioral health systems around the country have initiated efforts to transform their service systems by realigning their policies, services and structures to promote resilience and recovery. In the mental health arena, the work of the New Freedom Commission on Mental Health prompted much of this restructuring. Created in April of 2002, this Commission was charged with the task of examining the problems and gaps in mental health service delivery systems nationwide and recommending solutions to finally achieve the promise of "a life in the community" first made when the deinstitutionalization movement began half a century earlier.

Following several years of study and input from thousands of people nationwide, the Commission concluded that existing mental health systems were not organized to reach the single most important goal for people receiving services, the goal of recovery. To address that challenge, the Commission articulated the following vision:

> "We envision a future when everyone with a mental illness will recover, a future when mental illnesses are detected early, and a future when everyone with a mental illness at any stage of life has access to effective treatment and supports—essentials for living, working, learning and participating fully in the community" (DHHS, 2003).

Neither the Commission's findings nor its vision was surprising to many people receiving mental health care. Over the previous two decades, the nation's mental health consumer movement had grown and advocated just these kinds of changes in the nature of service delivery. What was new was that their vision of recovery and community inclusion had now been adopted by the nation's mental health system.

## New Recovery Advocacy Movement: Resources for a Lifetime Journey

While the transition from segregation and lifetime dependency to inclusion and capacity development took hold in the mental health field, a new recovery advocacy movement was unfolding within the addiction field. Champions of this movement have included people in recovery and their family members, addiction treatment providers and addiction researchers, all calling for sweeping changes in the way we envision, develop and deliver services to people with severe alcohol and other drug problems.

One of the most influential researchers and advocates in this new recovery advocacy movement has been William L. White. White maintains that, at its core, this movement represents a shift away from crisis-oriented, problem-focused and professionally directed models of care to a proactive, solution-focused approach directed by the person in recovery. It views addiction as a chronic illness and the recovery process as a lifetime journey that builds on people's strengths and resources, both internal and external. From this perspective, what is crucial is that people play active and central roles in choosing the services that will help them select and manage their own long-

---

[2] Details of the recovery movements and what they mean for both addiction and mental health services are offered in the Institute of Medicine's recently-released Improving the Quality of Health Care for Mental Health and Substance Use Conditions and in "A Conceptual Framework for Recovery in Philadelphia: History, Opportunities, and Implications for Practice"

term pathways and styles of recovery.[2] The recovery management approach to addiction that White describes is one of the cornerstones of Philadelphia's system-transformation efforts.

## Children's Behavioral Health: Focus on Resilience

In recent years there also has been a growing movement to change the nature of children's behavioral health care. Significant reports, including those of the Surgeon General, the New Freedom Commission on Mental Health, the Institute of Medicine and the World Health Organization, all reinforce the urgent need to foster behavioral health in children by embracing a public health approach that focuses on promoting resilience in children and families. According to the National Technical Assistance Center for Children's Mental Health, this type of approach is characterized by:

- a greater emphasis on building skills that enhance resilience and creating environments that promote and support optimal behavioral health;
- balancing the focus on children's behavioral health challenges with an equally strong focus on children's strengths;
- increasing the amount of collaboration across systems and sectors, including all settings and structures that affect children's well-being; and
- taking local needs and strengths into consideration in implementing services.

Similar to recovery-oriented services that build on the strengths of individuals, families and communities, resilience-promoting services are described as a departure from the field's traditional primary focus on the challenges and problems of children and families.

To provide the best services possible, prevention, treatment and community organizations must identify, nurture and develop the many internal and external conditions known as "protective factors." A concentration on these factors has greater potential for protection, healing and positive change than a narrow concentration on risks, adversities and stressors—factors which typically are much harder to change.

## *The Quality Chasm:* A Fundamental Redesign

The paradigm shift that is underway in behavioral health was further cemented by recommendations articulated in a series of reports by the Institute of Medicine (IOM) on improving the quality of health care. The most recent report, released in 2006, focuses on "improving the quality of healthcare for mental health and substance use conditions" by identifying ten rules to guide the redesign of healthcare. According to the IOM report, following the ten rules will require *"...a fundamental redesign of health care by health care organizations and delivery systems"* (2006, p. 56). These rules are outlined in Table 1, on the following page, with more detailed information available at http://www.iom.edu/Activities/Quality/MHQualityChasm.aspx.

**Table 1. Institute of Medicine's Ten Rules to Redesign and Improve Care**

1. Care based on healing relationships
2. Customization based on patient's needs and values
3. The patient as the source of control
4. Shared knowledge and the free flow of information
5. Evidence-based decision-making
6. Safety as a system property
7. The need for transparency
8. Anticipation of needs
9. Continuous decrease in waste
10. Cooperation among clinicians

In the following practice guidelines, these ten rules will be interwoven with the principles and values of health care reform, mental health transformation, the new recovery advocacy movement in addiction and the promotion of resilience in children's behavioral health.

## Local Momentum for Change

Along with the national trends that have informed this work, Philadelphia's efforts have unfolded against a backdrop of state-level support for and commitment to system transformation. In the 2005 report, *A Call for Change,* the Pennsylvania Department of Public Welfare, Office of Mental Health and Substance Abuse Services (OMHSAS) pledged to transform all service systems within the state to embrace a recovery orientation. The practice guidelines outlined in *Transformation of Behavioral Health in Philadelphia* are in keeping with the direction courageously laid out by OMHSAS in *A Call for Change.*

Finally, some of the most significant calls for change have come from both the people and families being served and the city's strong provider advocacy community. Philadelphia's providers have demonstrated their commitment to the idea that a true recovery- and resilience-oriented system of care does not simply add recovery support services to the existing treatment system. Rather, this transformation should have a profound impact on all the ways in which care is delivered, be it professional clinical care, rehabilitation or community-based support. The transformation process also extends beyond the behavioral health system to other people-serving systems, and to the broader community. Providers have also maintained that the radical and far-reaching reorientation of care that is envisioned—and the dramatically different outcomes that individuals and families deserve—will require sweeping changes in the way the administrative system "does business."

DBHIDS recognizes that transformation will have a significant impact on all stakeholders and processes, including the administrative infrastructure, and has been committed to transparent, participatory processes in the development of these guidelines. This commitment will remain strong throughout the implementation process. All stakeholders are invited to join these efforts and to lend their passion and their expertise to this challenging, rewarding and vitally important next step in the evolution of Philadelphia's behavioral health system.

# Section II: Overview of the Framework

## Philadelphia's Approach to Transformation

## The Practice Guidelines

## Components of the Framework

# Philadelphia's Approach to Transformation

Before examining the scope, purpose and framework of these guidelines, it is important to provide a brief overview of Philadelphia's approach to developing a system that promotes recovery and resilience, and to acknowledge the systemic challenges that exist.

## Integrated Service Approach

The Philadelphia Department of Behavioral Health and Intellectual disAbility Services (DBHIDS) is taking a holistic approach to the transformation of behavioral health care. This approach uses the concepts of recovery and resilience to form a conceptual framework for service delivery and a bridge in the integration of mental health and addiction services for children, adolescents, transition-age youths, adults and families. (Please refer to Appendix B for further discussion of the concepts of recovery and resilience).

This aspect of transformation is particularly important. Although mental health and substance use conditions frequently co-occur within the same individual, the services for these two categories of conditions are often disconnected and/or delivered in parallel or sequential service models. In Philadelphia, however, services for mental health and substance-related conditions are funded and overseen by the same agency. This offers the city the opportunity to bring these services, not only under the same roof, but also under the same vision and goal: that of resilience, recovery and a meaningful and self-determined life in the community.

## Transformative Approach

Three approaches to recovery-focused system transformation efforts have been identified: additive, selective and transformative approaches (Achara, Evans, & King, 2010). In an *additive approach*, systems focus on simply adding non-clinical recovery support services to the existing treatment system. As this approach focuses on adding new services, it perpetuates the belief that recovery-oriented systems of care can be created only with "new dollars."

Additive approaches to system transformation fail to recognize that all services, including treatment, should be delivered within a recovery framework. They overlook the essential role that treatment services must play in transformation processes. The primary focus in additive approaches is on recovery support services, rather than on re-examining **all** new and existing services through a new lens and values framework. As a result, important treatment variables such as assessment processes, service planning, the nature of service relationships and the focus of services remain unchanged.

This raises the risk that, even if non-clinical recovery support services are made available, they may be offered or designed in a manner that is not recovery oriented. They may be provided in ways that fail to reflect the values and principles of recovery-oriented care.

Another emerging approach to recovery-focused system transformation is the *selective approach*. In this approach, there is recognition that treatment practices must be changed and better aligned with principles of recovery and resilience, but the emphasis is on changing the treatment practices of select programs or in particular levels of care and incorporating recovery support services into the system.

Philadelphia's practice guidelines are based on a *transformative approach* to system change. In this approach, the entire system—including the context in which it operates—is aligned with principles of recovery and resilience. This includes treatment services and non-clinical recovery support services, as well as the fiscal, policy, community and social contexts within which the system operates.

In the transformative approach, the nature of treatment itself radically changes to align with the values and principles of recovery and resilience. Non-clinical recovery supports are developed and integrated into treatment settings and community contexts. Funding and regulatory policies are examined and modified through the lens of recovery- and resilience-oriented approaches. Non-clinical recovery supports and clinical treatment services are provided in a seamless, integrated manner and regarded, not only as equal in importance, but also as indispensable in promoting sustained recovery. To illustrate this approach, strategies that apply to both clinical and non-clinical recovery support services are interwoven throughout this document.

In Philadelphia's transformative approach, **there is no diminishing of the value or role of professional treatment.** In fact, as those working and those receiving services in the system focus on recovery as a real possibility, build resilience and remove barriers to a successful life in the community:

- motivation for change increases;
- acceptability of services increases;
- insight into the need for additional help increases; and, as a result,
- the demand for expert clinical care increases.

Along with increased demand come higher expectations of the skill and sophistication with which treatment professionals deliver care. For treatment providers whose traditions and/or funding mechanisms may have steered their focus of care toward deficit, disease and dysfunction, the shift to a focus on everyday functioning in the real world requires both an expansion and a deepening of the skills they already possess. Whether this practice incorporates cognitive-behavioral psychotherapy, family therapy, psychiatric rehabilitation strategies, psychopharmacology or any other approach, recovery- and resilience-oriented clinical care requires that the provider use the highest level of professional expertise, along with his or her unique personal experiences, to activate resilience factors and facilitate recovery. Philadelphia's approach to transformation embraces a number of critical elements of effective services, including evidence-based practices, trauma-informed services and attention to heath equity. (Please see Appendix C and Appendix D for descriptions of the roles of evidence-based practices and trauma-informed services in Philadelphia's approach to system transformation.)

To reflect the transformative approach, this document is written in terms of "recovery- and/or resilience-oriented services," a concept that encompasses *both* clinical and non-clinical services.

## The Systemic Challenges

On the national level, behavioral health systems stand at a challenging point in history, a time of in which financial constraints are changing the nature and availability of funding opportunities and setting new standards for quality, cost-effectiveness and accountability:

- the Affordable Care Act (ACA) and other healthcare trends are challenging providers to adapt to a rapidly changing healthcare landscape in order to improve outcomes and quality, as well as reduce spending; and

- funding and reimbursement mechanisms are being retooled to require and reward successful management of chronic conditions and prevention of recurrence, often through a proactive focus on wellness, preventive approaches and community-based services and supports.

With its foundation in the empowerment of individuals, families and communities to support resilience and long-term recovery, Philadelphia's transformation process is already in strong conceptual alignment with the spirit of healthcare reform. Providers who have embraced a recovery-oriented approach may not yet use the same terminology as those who are well versed in the ACA, but the implications for practice are the same.

It is important to acknowledge these challenges and opportunities, because they have the potential to affect all that the stakeholders in this system are doing now—as well as all they dream of doing in the future. However, much of what is proposed here does not require additional resources. Rather, it requires a reorientation of services and a focus on long-term recovery and resilience as the desired outcomes. In addition, the directions proposed in these guidelines allow providers enough latitude to respond creatively and flexibly to both the threats and the opportunities of the day. In fact, this document is based on the premise that a transformed system is even more essential in the face of social challenges and funding constraints. This is because:

- transformation can better equip individuals and families to face their challenges by connecting them with both formal and informal supports and services;
- transformation emphasizes the effectiveness and efficiency of services; and
- a transformed system also works to capitalize on the previously untapped resources of the people receiving services in the system—people who have many valuable resources to offer one another, providers and the city as a whole.

It is also essential to acknowledge that many of the values and principles described in this document are already embraced by many providers in Philadelphia. Unfortunately, the systems at the local, state and federal levels are not yet fully aligned to support the delivery of services that promote recovery and resilience. Consequently, implementation of some of the strategies outlined in this document will require continued fiscal and policy alignment with recovery and resilience principles. This reality will be acknowledged frequently throughout the document.

Despite the legitimate challenges that exist, this system and its stakeholders have already begun to align their practices with those driven by recovery and resilience. This will ensure that all children, youth, adults and families receiving behavioral health care in Philadelphia have access to the services and supports they need to live meaningful and self-determined lives in this vibrant community. The practice guidelines contained in this document serve as one more tool to turn this shared vision into a reality.

# Section II: Overview of the Framework

# The Practice Guidelines

## Scope of the Guidelines

In keeping with the comprehensive system-transformation efforts that have begun in the health care arena, the guidelines outlined in this document are meant to help providers implement services and supports that promote resilience, recovery and wellness in children, youth, adults and families. They apply to all treatment providers and all levels of care. However, they are not intended to encapsulate all possible services or supports that promote recovery and resilience. **The strategies in this document are merely *examples* of the types of activities and services that providers can implement**.

The guidelines have direct implications for staff in all roles, including:

- people with clinical training (including psychiatrists, nurses, psychologists, social workers, rehabilitation practitioners, counselors and supervisors);
- people who provide case management and/or provide peer support and mentoring; and
- people who provide various forms of support, including clerical, technical and maintenance staff.

The term "staff" is used to refer to all individuals who are reimbursed for working in a provider organization. This includes psychiatrists, recovery coaches, peer specialists, psychologists, social workers, mental health and addiction counselors, case managers, administrative support staff, etc.

The guidelines in this document are targeted only at providers of behavioral health treatment. However, prevention services constitute another critically important part of a comprehensive system of care that promotes recovery and resilience. The implications of a recovery and resilience orientation for prevention services will be explored in an upcoming document in this series.

## Purpose of the Guidelines

Many of the strategies contained in this document are drawn from the collective experiences of stakeholders in Philadelphia. They are not new inventions, but reflections and extensions of innovative practices and lessons learned in communities throughout Philadelphia. Many examples of these innovations exist throughout the system, and these practice guidelines—and the many individuals and families who may benefit from them—owe much to the dedication and ingenuity of those who have designed and carried out these initiatives.

It is important that the reader understand that the strategies contained in this document are not intended to be a laundry list of new activities that must now be incorporated into all service settings. Understanding the four service domains and the seven goals of services is the most critical task. The suggested strategies are examples of the kinds of activities that can help organizations and providers achieve these goals. These strategies should be modified and adopted based on the preferences, cultures and needs of people being served and the community context in which they live.

The guidelines are also not intended to focus exclusively on the delivery of new services, but to align existing services within a framework of shared vision and values. Where new approaches that would require additional funding are identified, DBHIDS will work in partnership with stakeholders to develop fiscal and policy strategies that will allow for their implementation.

In short, these guidelines are intended to:

- document the shared vision that has emerged in the system;
- create a common language for all stakeholders;
- provide concrete strategies to assist treatment providers in developing and implementing services that promote recovery and resilience;
- be a tool that providers can use to have ongoing dialogue with their staff;
- serve as a catalyst for continued dialogue between DBHIDS and all stakeholders, in which they further refine thoughts about the types of services and supports that are most effective;
- create specific areas of focus for the continued alignment of the administrative infrastructure of the system;
- provide a lens through which DBHIDS can manage the City behavioral health system; and
- represent a milestone in our collective efforts and launch the next phase of Philadelphia's system transformation process.

An understanding of these guidelines must also include a recognition of the functions they are **not** intended to fulfill. For example:

- This document is not designed to promote a "one-size-fits-all" model that should be applied universally across programs, levels of care and staff. Some of the strategies will be more relevant to or appropriate for particular levels of care, populations or staff. Providers are encouraged to work collaboratively with staff and the people they serve to determine the strategies that best fit their settings and communities.
- These guidelines should not be construed as a rigid monitoring tool against which providers will be held accountable. This document contains more than 700 examples of potential strategies, far more

than any single program might implement. The diversity reflected in the variety of strategies is consistent with the recognition that there are multiple pathways to recovery and resilience. It would not be feasible or realistic to use this document as a rigid monitoring tool. Instead, the document will be the primary tool used to inform the development of performance improvement and credentialing strategies. In collaboration with providers, DBHIDS will identify some of the core strategies that are essential to providing services and supports that promote resilience and recovery. Those core strategies will form the foundation of future performance improvement and credentialing processes.

- This document is not intended to replace the practice guidelines developed by professional associations (e.g., those of the American Psychiatric Association). The guidelines contained in this document are intended to supplement existing professional guidelines as well as integrate local lessons learned and the latest thinking in the behavioral health field.

- These guidelines do not represent a static, finished product. It is anticipated that strategies will be further refined as the dialogue continues and new lessons are learned. Going forward, some strategies may be removed, others may be altered, and new strategies may be added. This document is intended to bring a sharper focus to this work, and in doing so will inevitably lead to changes in the document itself.

## Next Steps

It is clear that the practice guidelines do not yet describe the system as it is, but set a vision and clear direction for practice in a system that is emerging and will continue to evolve.

One of the most valuable lessons of our field's history is that services do not take place in a vacuum. The success of any service-improvement effort relies on active support from the overall system that sustains it, and from the larger community that gives it a home. Fully integrating these practices into the system—and into people's lives—will require significant changes in the fiscal, policy, regulatory and community contexts.

So, while this document focuses on practices needed in service and support settings, two additional documents will be developed detailing the changes needed in other settings:

- The next document in this series will describe the changes that are necessary in the overall system to support the implementation of these practices. These will include fiscal, policy, performance improvement, credentialing and evaluation strategies.

- The final document in this series will focus on the role of the community in promoting recovery and resilience. That document will be written in the context of the emerging federal direction around the critical role of the community in prevention, early intervention and the promotion of overall health.

As was the case in the development of these guidelines for providers, the guidelines that target system and community contexts will also be developed through transparent, participatory processes. In addition, the insight of diverse stakeholders will be particularly critical in identifying needs, realities, potential barriers to implementation and strategies for addressing them.

Following the dissemination of this guidelines document, DBHIDS will host a series of focus groups with all stakeholders, to explore barriers to implementation. Given the systemic barriers that tend to prevent transformative change, DBHIDS will work collaboratively with providers to identify policy and fiscal strategies that can be aligned locally, as well as those that will require additional alignment at state or federal levels. These focus groups will also create a mechanism to identify the core goals and strategies that will inform performance improvement and credentialing processes in the future.

# Components of the Framework

The framework for these practice guidelines includes:

- ten core values that have guided the development of transformation principles and strategies and will continue to guide the implementation process;
- four service domains in which the strategies will be carried out; and
- seven concrete, action-oriented goals that organize and focus the strategies.

## Core Values

Each of the ten core values that drive this framework is supported by principles rooted in research, and in the collective experience of individuals, families, providers and service systems.

The core values were drawn from the earlier work of the Recovery Advisory Committee and from the values identified in the report issued by the Mayor's Blue Ribbon Commission on Children's Behavioral Health. The list was further developed through the work of stakeholders in the Summer of 2009.

1. Strength-based Approaches that Promote Hope: A strengths perspective is woven throughout these system-transformation efforts. Services are focused on identifying and building strengths, assets, resources and protective factors within the individual, family, peer group and community, rather than focusing solely on identifying and addressing problems or challenges in the individual's or family's life. These strengths are mobilized to support the individual's and the family's journey to wellness. A focus on hope is equally essential—the message that people can and do show resilience in the face of adversity, and can and do recover from behavioral health conditions. Change is always possible, and the extent to which people's lives can change is often beyond what we can imagine. We learn hope by seeing others lead meaningful lives in their communities, listening to their stories and having opportunities to give to others. Hope-inducing environments can help people of all ages in their recovery processes.

2. Community Inclusion, Partnership and Collaboration: The focus of care is on integrating individuals and families into the larger life of their communities, connecting with the support and hospitality of the community, developing community resources that support recovery and resilience and encouraging service contributions to and from the larger community. Resilience, recovery and wellness can be tapped, initiated,

catalyzed and promoted in care settings, but can be maintained only in the context of people's natural environments. Connecting services, individuals and families with the community is no longer considered optional, but is understood as an integral factor in sustaining wellness.

3.   Person- and family-directed approaches: In recovery- and resilience-oriented systems, service designs shift from an expert model to a partnership/consultation model, in which everyone's perspective, experience and expertise is welcomed and considered. Each person's and each family's values, needs and preferences are respected and considered central to any decision-making process. Services and supports are individualized, built with and around each person and family. All parties in the system recognize that there are many pathways to recovery and that people have a right to choose their own paths. People have the opportunity to choose from a diverse menu of services and supports and to participate in all decisions that affect their lives and those of their children. Multidisciplinary teams that include participants and family members reduce fragmentation and ensure the delivery of comprehensive, effective services.

4.   Family Inclusion and Leadership: Family members are actively engaged and involved at all levels of the service process. Families—and particularly parents of children and youth—are seen as an integral part of policy development, planning, service delivery and service evaluation. Assessment and service planning are family focused. The system and its providers recognize that families come in many varieties. Families of birth, foster and adoptive families and families of choice are respected, valued and involved in meaningful ways. When multiple family members are involved in care in different programs and agencies, providers take steps to ensure that services are integrated.

5.   Peer Culture, Support and Leadership: Service systems and providers recognize the power of peer support and affirm that recognition by: a) creating environments in which peers can support one another in formal and informal ways and providing opportunities for that support; b) hiring people to provide peer support to individuals and/or families; c) ensuring representation of youth and people in recovery at all levels of the system; d) developing respectful, collaborative relationships between behavioral health agencies and the service structures of local recovery mutual-aid societies and assertively linking people to peer-based support services (e.g., mutual/self-help groups, other recovery community support institutions and informal peer support); e) acknowledging the role that sharing stories of lived experience can play in helping others initiate and sustain the recovery process; and f) developing opportunities for people in recovery and youth to engage in active leadership roles at all levels of the system.

6.   Person-First (Culturally Competent) Approaches: The title of this core

value reflects the fact that services that are appropriate to and respectful of culture—often referred to as "culturally competent"—must also respect the individuality and centrality of each unique individual. In a person-first (culturally competent) service system, all staff and volunteers are able to work effectively with individuals and families from different cultures. They possess knowledge of the values, worldviews and practices of the major cultural groups they serve—and, equally important, the humility to know the limits of their knowledge. They address culture broadly, not forgetting the importance of ethnicity, nation of birth and primary language, but also acknowledging the implications of gender, age, sexual orientation, religion, socioeconomic factors and other key characteristics. Rather than merely developing a generic understanding of the people they serve, however, they are also skilled at using cultural knowledge to develop an accurate and individualized understanding of each person they serve, each family and each community. Providers also possess an understanding of their own cultural worldview, the ways in which it enriches their work and the ways in which it may constrain their work.

7.  Trauma-Informed Approaches: All components of the service system are designed with an understanding of the role that serious adverse experiences can play in the lives of individuals and families. Services are delivered in safe and trustworthy environments and through respectful, nurturing relationships, to promote healing and avoid inadvertent re-traumatization. Individuals and families are always assessed for the extent to which the spectrum of traumatic experiences may have affected their lives and their ability to participate safely in care and establish recovery. They are offered services and supports that will help them reduce the destructive effects of traumatic experiences and maximize the growth that can emerge from the healing process.

8.  Holistic Approaches toward Care: Services and supports are designed to enhance the development of the whole person. Care transcends a narrow focus on symptom reduction and promotes wellness as a key component of all care. In attending to the whole person, there is an emphasis on exploring and addressing primary care needs in an integrated manner. Providers and peers also explore, mobilize and address spirituality, sexuality and other dimensions of wellness in service settings.

9.  Care for the Needs and Safety of Children and Adolescents: Service systems and providers recognize the incredible resilience of children and adolescents, along with their unique vulnerabilities and the complexities that attend their need for services and support. As a result, providers employ a developmental approach in the delivery of services. Like adults, children and their families are shown respect and given a partnership role in services and supports. Screening and assessment

processes are informed by knowledge of the ways in which children's and adolescents' strengths, symptoms, needs and progress tend to differ from those of adults, and of ways in which those differences can be honored. Providers also recognize that attention to the safety, needs and well being of children and adolescents includes attention to the safety, needs and well being of their families—and back up that recognition with concrete action.

10. Partnership and Transparency: This system-transformation effort is built upon the values of transparency and partnership at all levels of the system. This applies to the ways in which system administrators strive to work with providers, as well as the ways in which providers aim to collaborate with the individuals and families receiving services.

Though the core values are too global to represent action-oriented strategies that people can pick up and use, it is essential for all service providers to understand and embrace these values and the principles that support them. These core values are made operational in the strategies that follow in Section III, with multiple values often driving the same strategy.

## Service Domains

Stakeholders have identified four service domains that are essential components of a recovery- and resilience-oriented behavioral health system:

1. **Assertive Outreach and Initial Engagement:** The many obstacles people face in entering and staying in services make this domain essential to the success of the system and the people it seeks to serve. Human tragedy has shown that many people die before they receive the help they need, but empirically supported practices have given us many ways of increasing motivation; eliminating obstacles; and making services more accessible, more acceptable and easier to navigate.

2. **Screening, Assessment, Service Planning and Service Delivery:** There is a wealth of concepts and resources that can be used to make care more effective and to lay a better foundation for ongoing recovery. These include emphases on individual, family and community strengths, and on resilience and recovery capital, from the initial screening and assessment process through the interventions chosen. These emphases also extend to the integration of services for mental health, primary care, substance use and trauma-related issues and the mobilization of professional and community-based recovery support structures from the earliest days of treatment.

3. **Continuing Support and Early Re-intervention:** Although recovery is a significant reality, some behavioral health challenges are chronic conditions that can move into and out of remission. Effective professional, peer and community support can, not only help individuals and families

achieve their dreams and goals, but also prevent, identify and address recurrence of the symptoms of mental health and substance-related challenges. This support can take many forms and occur at many times throughout the recovery process.

4. **Community Connection and Mobilization:** The forging of a meaningful life in the community must be driven by the true hopes and dreams of individuals and families—hopes and dreams that may have been worn down by years, decades or even generations of poverty, prejudice, trauma, illness and hopelessness. Traditionally seen as sources of danger, temptation and deprivation surrounding the treatment refuge, communities must instead be seen for and cultivated as sources of support, fellowship, civic engagement and healing. Behavioral health organizations and providers must recapture their roles as members of and contributors to their communities, so they can foster the exchange of resources between those communities and the individuals and families they serve.

## Goals

To make these practice guidelines useful for real human beings doing real work, the action-oriented strategies within each of the four domains have been organized under seven functional goals.

A. Provide integrated services
B. Create an atmosphere that promotes strength, recovery and resilience
C. Develop inclusive, collaborative service teams and processes
D. Provide services, training and supervision that promote recovery and resilience
E. Provide individualized services to identify and address barriers to wellness
F. Achieve successful outcomes through empirically informed approaches
G. Promote recovery and resilience through evaluation and quality-improvement processes

The table on the following page illustrates the ways in which all of the elements of this framework intersect.

The final and practical product of this document is the collection of strategies presented in Section III, "Strategies in the Four Domains," that can serve as concrete, action-oriented guidelines for service transformation. That section includes a chapter for the strategies in each of the four service domains.

# The Framework

## 4 DOMAINS

**1:** Assertive outreach and initial engagement

**2:** Screening, assessment, service planning & service delivery

**3:** Continuing support and early Re-intervention

**4:** Community connection and mobilization

## 7 GOALS

A. Provide integrated services

B. Create an atmosphere that promotes strength, recovery and resilience

C. Develop inclusive, collaborative service teams and processes

D. Provide services, training and supervision that promote recovery and resilience

E. Provide individualized services to identify and address barriers to wellness

F. Achieve successful outcomes through empirically informed approaches

G. Promote recovery and resilience through evaluation and quality improvement

## 10 CORE VALUES

In each domain, all of the goals for the delivery of effective care are pursued through strategies. Each of these strategies reflects one or more of the ten core values that drive this work:

1. Strength-based approaches that promote hope

2. Community inclusion, partnership and collaboration

3. Person and family-directed approaches

4. Family inclusion and leadership

5. Peer culture, support and leadership

6. Person-first (culturally competent) approaches

7. Trauma-informed approaches

8. Holistic approaches toward care

9. Care for the needs and safety of children and adolescents

10. Partnership and transparency

**Transformation Practice Guidelines**
Philadelphia DBHIDS

# Section III: Strategies in the Four Domains

**Using this Section**

**Domain 1: Assertive Outreach and Initial Engagement**

**Domain 2: Screening, Assessment, Service Planning and Service Delivery**

**Domain 3: Continuing Support and Early Re-intervention**

**Domain 4: Community Connection and Mobilization**

# Section III: Strategies in the Four Domains

# Using This Section

As mentioned in the previous section, Section III offers a collection of action-oriented strategies that organizations and individual staff members can use to:

- build their capacity to provide resilience- and recovery-oriented services; and
- work toward transforming organizations, services and the lives of the individuals and families they serve.

## The Four Domains

This section is organized in four chapters which all follow the same basic structure: After a brief, bulleted "Domain Overview," each Domain begins with a brief "Background and Rationale" portion that summarizes some of the trends that have led us here and some of the evidence that points toward the need for attention to recovery- and resilience-oriented care in this domain.

The remainder of each chapter consists of seven bulleted lists of strategies, one for each of the seven goals:

A.  Provide integrated services
B.  Create an atmosphere that promotes strength, resilience and recovery
C.  Develop inclusive, collaborative service teams and processes
D.  Provide services, training and supervision that promote recovery and resilience
E.  Provide individualized services to identify and address barriers to wellness
F.  Achieve successful outcomes through empirically supported approaches
G.  Promote recovery and resilience through evaluation and quality improvement

These strategies have been developed based on the contributions of many stakeholders, and on the growing body of literature on recovery- and resilience-oriented systems. To show the importance of these strategies to the well being of the individuals and families they will affect, each strategy is followed by a reference to the core value or values it reflects. To avoid redundancy and keep the practice guidelines at a reasonable length, many strategies that are effective in multiple domains are presented only in the first of the appropriate domains, rather than repeated in each of these domains.

Given the commitment and wisdom of stakeholders in these processes, there is no doubt that the seeds sown in the following pages will give rise to many connections, many new ideas, and many enhancements of these offerings.

# Section III: Strategies in the Four Domains

# Domain 1: Assertive Outreach and Initial Engagement

## Domain Overview

Ensure timely access to services for children, adults and families in need of behavioral health care and supports.

- Identify and bring individuals in need of treatment into services
- Increase access to services by removing barriers
- Enhance approaches to engagement in services
- Increase retention in services

# Section III: Strategies in the Four Domains

# Domain 1: Assertive Outreach and Initial Engagement

## Background and Rationale

Each year, only about 10 percent of the people whose conditions meet the criteria for substance use disorders receive specialty behavioral health care (SAMHSA, 2003). While the percentage is somewhat higher for mental health, only about 45 percent of people who experience serious psychological stress indicative of mental illness receive specialty care in a given year (SAMHSA, 2006).

Data on children and youth provide even greater cause for concern:

- A review of three longitudinal studies concluded that close to 40 percent of young people have had at least one behavioral health disorder by the time they are 16 years of age (Institute of Medicine, 2009).

- Prevention, early identification and early intervention activities are increasingly seen as critical for children, but 75 percent of children with behavioral health challenges have no contact with children's service systems (Institute of Medicine, 2009).

- The discrepancy between the need for and the use of services is highest among minority youth (Harrison, 2004).

Individuals and families who do seek behavioral health services generally do so in the later stages of problem development (Hser et al., 1997). However, research on both mental health and substance use disorders indicates that the earlier in the course of the illness an intervention is initiated, the better the prognosis for long-term recovery (Melle, 2004; Moos & Moos, 2003).

The belief that individuals and families cannot be engaged successfully unless they are "ready" or "motivated" for treatment pervades much of traditional behavioral health care. This belief has been carried down in addiction treatment folklore, such as the idea that people need "to hit bottom" before they will be receptive to help. In mental health, there has been the assertion that "we shouldn't be working harder for clients than they are willing to work themselves." Statements such as these convey the belief that people have to prove they are ready for help, either through the intensity of their pain or through their demonstration of effort. Through much of the field's history, this stance has reduced the extent to which people are successfully engaged in services in a timely way by delaying care until the person and/or family has little choice but come into contact with the service system. As a result, systems have been primarily reactive to crises.

Systems of care that promote recovery and resilience engage people in services and supports at earlier stages of problem development, thus preventing further damage and deepening of behavioral health conditions. Such systems provide multiple points of access, so they are no longer seen as the option of last resort. And although motivation continues to be viewed as an important factor, it is considered an outcome of the service relationship rather than a prerequisite for treatment (White, 2008). In other words, helping individuals and families become motivated for change is now seen as an appropriate and important task for providers early in the course of treatment.

Unfortunately, among those adults, families and youth who do eventually gain access to care—often in crisis—many do not return after the first appointment, and others drop out of care prematurely (e.g., as soon as the crisis resolves). For both adults and youth, leaving treatment prematurely is associated with poor outcomes. Individuals, families and youth have better outcomes if they remain connected to behavioral health services and supports until they have established a firm foundation for sustained wellness (Wallace & Weeks, 2004).

Recovery- and resilience-oriented systems of care work deliberately to improve initial engagement through a number of strategies, some of which are deceptively simple but can still bring about significant success. For example, the use of intensive family-focused telephone engagement strategies has been associated with a 50% decrease in initial no-show rates and a 24% decrease in early service termination (Szapocznik, 1988). Focusing on the most pressing priorities of the individual and family at the outset of treatment can also ensure that services are perceived as helpful and relevant.

The many challenges to access, engagement and retention in care are frustrating, not only for individuals and families in need of services, but also for providers. Behavioral health providers in our nation work in progressively rigid systems whose policies, funding streams and regulations increasingly limit the scope of services they can offer. While many providers have developed innovative programs in spite of systemic barriers, these programs are often difficult to sustain without the necessary fiscal and policy alignment. DBHIDS will work collaboratively with providers to address the systemic barriers to implementing strategies that promote assertive outreach and engagement.

The recovery transformation proposed in these practice guidelines represents an opportunity to align all levels of the system, with the overarching goal of promoting recovery and resilience. It is the belief of stakeholders in Philadelphia that systems of care that promote recovery and resilience:

- focus on outreach, engagement and ways of enhancing people's motivation to initiate and sustain treatment;
- design early intervention activities to identify children's behavioral health challenges earlier in life and earlier in the course of problem development; and
- identify effective ways of keeping individuals and families engaged in a variety of services and supports until they believe they have achieved their personal goals for health and wellness.

# Domain 1: Assertive Outreach and Initial Engagement

## Goal A: Provide Integrated Services

**Objective:** Establish collaborative relationships with primary care providers to facilitate outreach and engagement and increase access to care

Potential Strategies:

- **Establish partnerships in a variety of health care settings** that will facilitate the use of empirically supported behavioral health screening; early intervention; and referral strategies in primary care settings, e.g., hospitals, ambulatory health clinics, community health centers, school and college health clinics. *(Community inclusion, partnership and collaboration; Holistic approaches toward care)*

- **Partner with primary care to create on-site assessment and referral services** within primary care settings, wherever possible and appropriate. *(Holistic approaches toward care)*

- **Establish partnerships with pediatricians to include a behavioral health component in wellness checks,** to normalize behavioral health care and to facilitate early intervention. *(Care for the needs and safety of children and adolescents)*

- **Address co-occurring physical illness in integrated ways,** through assertive referral to and coordination with primary care providers, and aim to address co-occurring illnesses through integrated services rather than consecutive care. *(Holistic approaches toward care)*

**Objective:** Establish collaborative relationships with community-based supports to increase engagement and access to diverse services and supports

Potential Strategies:

- **Collaborate with local childcare centers to facilitate early intervention.** Increase awareness of developmental milestones and the behavioral health services that are available to address children's developmental delays and emotional or behavioral challenges. *(Care for the needs and safety of children and adolescents)*

- **Form partnerships with the natural sources of support** that underserved populations are most likely to seek out for help. For example, historically disempowered groups such as people of color often turn to faith-based organizations, grassroots groups, indigenous healers and community leaders in times of distress. *(Person-first [culturally competent] approaches; Community inclusion, partnership* *and collaboration)*

- **Connect with key community organizations** that intersect with individuals at risk. These might include housing and food shelters, halfway houses, church-based meal programs, community corrections facilities, recreation centers, etc. *(Community inclusion, partnership and collaboration)*

- **Develop partnerships with existing peer support programs, recovery community organizations** and mutual aid support groups: Identify local organizations that provide peer support to individuals and families, such as the National Alliance on Mental Illness (NAMI), Alcoholics Anonymous, Narcotics Anonymous and ProAct, and assertively connect people to appropriate resources early in care. *(Peer culture, support and leadership)*

- **Identify and partner with organizations that provide other resources** that may be beneficial for the individuals and families you serve. These might include local community centers, fitness facilities, local small businesses, etc. *(Community inclusion, partnership and collaboration)*

**Objective:** Promote earlier problem recognition through collaborative relationships with safety-oriented and other service systems

**Potential Strategies:**

- **Form partnerships and learning exchanges with first responders** (e.g., police, fire, paramedics, other emergency services) to provide education on mental health issues, substance use disorders and common responses to trauma; facilitate referrals; and alert them to the types of situations you might be able to help them stabilize. *(Community inclusion, partnership and collaboration; Trauma-informed approaches)*

- **Form partnerships and learning exchanges with Child Protective Services,** to facilitate cross training and referrals. *(Care for the needs and safety of children; Trauma-informed approaches)*

- **Collaborate with community partners on identification of children's needs,** including recreation centers, child welfare and juvenile justice organizations to provide services to children who are experiencing behavioral health challenges. *(Community inclusion, partnership and collaboration; Care for the needs and safety of children and adolescents)*

- **Follow a "no wrong door" policy for children, adolescents and adults,** to engage individuals at whatever point they enter the system, and determine the most appropriate type and level of care at that time. This is particularly important for children seeking help (Mayor's Blue Ribbon Commission, 2007). Refer to agencies with additional levels of care as appropriate, and shepherd children and families through these transitions. *(Community inclusion, partnership and collaboration; Care for the needs and safety of children and adolescents)*

> *"Children should not have to fail a level of care before they are connected to the right services."*
> *—Provider*

# Domain 1: Assertive Outreach and Initial Engagement

## Goal B: Create an Atmosphere that Promotes Strength, Recovery and Resilience

**Objective:** Create welcoming environments

**Potential Strategies:**

- **Make entry into care easier and more welcoming** by ensuring that entry points into care are streamlined, inviting and responsive to people's concerns, so they inspire hope and offer accurate and accessible information about the assistance that is available. *(Strength-based approaches that promote hope; Person-first [culturally competent] approaches)*

- **Train all staff in welcoming techniques.** For example, ensure that all staff answer the telephone in an engaging and respectful manner that demonstrates their commitment to being of service. *(Strength-based approaches that promote hope; Person-first [culturally competent] approaches)*

  > *"People are coming in at the bottom. Staff need to be friendly and culturally competent."*
  > —Person in Recovery

- **Use volunteer greeters** to serve in welcoming/ greeting roles. *(Strength-based approaches that promote hope; Person-first [culturally competent] approaches; Peer culture, support and leadership)*

- **Create welcoming waiting areas** that are culturally appropriate (e.g., with reading material, pictures, etc. that reflect the populations served). Ensure that the waiting area is family-friendly, with toys, coloring books and videos to engage children. *(Strength-based approaches that promote hope; Person-first [culturally competent] approaches; Family inclusion and leadership)*

**Objective:** Create environments that promote a sense of hope

**Potential Strategies:**

- **Create an organizational culture that reflects and sustains hope.** Begin building hope from the first contact. Even before they enter care, raise individuals' and families' expectations of positive outcomes by promoting increased hope (Woods, 1997). *(Strength-based approaches that promote hope; Person-first [culturally competent] approaches)*

- **Focus on resilience and recovery** in language, attitudes and practices. Reflect a culture that elicits and celebrates resilience and recovery rather than focusing on deficits. *(Strength-based approaches that promote hope; Person-first [culturally competent] approaches)*

- **In waiting rooms, show videos of success** that highlight youth, adults and families who have overcome behavioral health challenges (e.g., Philadelphia Transformation Video). *(Strength-based approaches that promote hope)*
- **Harness staff charisma and engagement skills** by using the most charismatic and engaging staff to conduct intake interviews and orientation seminars (Connors et al., 2002). *(Strength-based approaches that promote hope; Person-first [culturally competent] approaches)*

**Objective:** Create an organization-wide sense of mutual respect

**Potential Strategies:**

- **Adopt a "person-first" approach to service delivery,** and convey this approach to all staff and volunteers through training, supervision, mentorship and evaluation (for more specific guidelines on "person-first" approaches to services, please see the document entitled *Person First Assessment and Person Directed Planning* at http://www.dbhids.org/assets/Forms--Documents/personFirst.pdf). *(Person-first [culturally competent] approaches; Person- and family-directed approaches)*
- **View participants as people first and foremost**, with such issues as diagnoses, presenting problems and psychosocial history playing an important but secondary role. *(Strength-based approaches that promote hope; Person-first [culturally competent] approaches; Person- and family-directed approaches)*
- **Use person-first language** such as "a person with schizophrenia" rather than "a schizophrenic," or "a person with an addiction" rather than "an addict." *(Person-first [culturally competent] approaches; Person- and family-directed approaches)*
- **Promote an organization-wide sense of equality.** Promote and convey a conviction that each participant and family member has a life and is a fellow human being and equal, inside and outside the service setting. *(Strength-based approaches that promote hope; Person-first [culturally competent] approaches; Person- and family-directed approaches)*

# Domain 1: Assertive Outreach and Initial Engagement

## Goal C: Develop Inclusive, Collaborative Service Teams and Processes

**Objective:** Use the skills and experience of staff and volunteers strategically in outreach and initial engagement efforts

Potential Strategies:

- **Recruit outreach and intake staff with first-person experience.** Recruit staff with experiences of behavioral health challenges and recovery who have a special ability to engage with individuals and families; connect people to treatment and other recovery support services; and convey a sense of hope through the example of their own perseverance and success. Rather than waiting for individuals and families to seek behavioral health care in later stages of problem development, use assertive outreach to meet people at their current stages of change and in their natural environments *(Strength-based approaches that promote hope; Peer culture, support and leadership)*

- **Use peers in outreach efforts.** Sow the seeds of the collaborative process in the outreach and early engagement processes, through the use of peer specialists and recovery/wellness coaches. *(Strength-based approaches that promote hope; Peer culture, support and leadership)*

- **Use family peer support staff and volunteers in outreach efforts.** Develop a family peer support role, using volunteers or paid staff, focused on engaging families in services, helping staff identify families' basic transition needs and monitoring the fulfillment of those needs. Train and supervise staff and volunteers in reaching out to identified family members and key allies *(Family inclusion and leadership; Peer culture, support and leadership)*

> *The Mayor's Blue Ribbon Commission on Children's Behavioral Health (2007) endorsed the need to* "create mechanisms for a youth and family peer component to be integrated into all behavioral health care services for children and youth" *(Recommendation 2:3).*

**Objective:** Ensure that staff use effective processes for engaging families

Potential Strategies:

- **Identify and involve safe families and allies.** Early in the engagement process, obtain release forms that will facilitate engagement of safe family members and allies, and follow this process with phone outreach. Explain to family members and allies the resources, services and supports available to them at the agency and in the broader community. *(Family inclusion and leadership; Peer culture, support and leadership)*

- **Promote early contact with safe families and allies.** With children, or with adult participants' consent, contact safe family members and allies by phone as soon as possible, to:

  - **Answer any questions they might have**
  - **Seek collateral information about the participant and about family-related strengths and needs** *(Family inclusion and leadership; Care for the needs and safety of children and adolescents)*
  - **Ask for their involvement and support as the participant desires. (Family Resource Network, 2010).** *(Family inclusion and leadership; Person- and family-directed approaches)*

- **Coordinate initial telephone and in-person interviews with families.** Combine telephone and in-person initial interviews, a practice that has been associated with a 16%-to-25% increase in attendance rates (McKay et al., 1998). *(Family inclusion and leadership; Strength-based approaches that promote hope)*

> *"Have communication with the family prior to the first visit; have someone call to break the ice; have that person greet you when you arrive at the program. [They should] start the process before you walk through the door."*
> —Family Member

# Domain 1: Assertive Outreach and Initial Engagement

## Goal D: Provide Services, Training and Supervision that Promote Recovery and Resilience

**Objective:** Ensure that staff offer a menu of resources to facilitate engagement

Potential Strategies:

- **Make a range of services and supports available.** From the beginning, offer a diverse range of services and supports from which individuals and families can select to meet their unique needs and preferences. *(Person- and family-directed approaches; Person-first [culturally competent] approaches; Holistic approaches toward care)*

- **Evaluate the need for culture-specific services** that are tailored to or sensitive to the needs of participants' cultures or demographic factors (e.g., culture and/or gender-specific services). *(Person-first [culturally competent] approaches; Person- and family-directed approaches)*

- **Offer early connections with peer mentors.** As soon as they request services, offer to connect individuals and families with peer mentors. *(Strength-based approaches that promote hope; Peer culture, support and leadership)*

> *"Offer a Parent Advocate to a new family member, and let the advocate work with the parents."*
> *—Parent*

- **Offer to screen children** of adults and siblings of children and adolescents who are receiving services, in order to identify risks, challenges and the need for preventive or behavioral health services and support. *(Care for the needs and safety of children and adolescents; Trauma-informed approaches)*

**Objective:** Ensure that staff and volunteers place relationship first during initial engagement efforts

Potential Strategies:

- **Communicate consistently that relationships come first.** Communicate to outreach and intake staff, volunteers, participants, families and communities that a collaborative service and recovery relationship is a top priority of the organization, its representatives and the system as a whole, and ensure that staff have relevant training and supervision. For example, initial sessions should focus on relationship building rather than on completing paperwork. *(Person-first [culturally competent] approaches; Strength-based* *approaches that promote hope)*

- **Ensure that traditional boundaries do not get in the way of building strong therapeutic relationships.** Wherever it is safe and appropriate, re-think traditional notions of ethics and professional boundaries to encompass a more collaborative philosophy of care. Ensure that boundaries protect all involved, including the participant, the family, the volunteer or staff member and the organization. *(Person-first [culturally competent] approaches; Trauma-informed approaches)*

- **Respect participants' space and timing.** Find ways of entering into another person's life based on his or her "invitation" (and at his or her own pace), rather than on coercion, threat or agency mandates (except when serious risk exists). *(Person-first [culturally competent] approaches)*

- **Promote a focus on the story.** Focus initial sessions on the individual's and the family's story, rather than just on symptoms or problems. *(Strength-based approaches that promote hope; Person-first [culturally competent] approaches)*

**Objective: Ensure that staff and volunteers cultivate and communicate openness and humility**

**Potential Strategies:**

> *"We can deal with you not knowing something—being new to the field, for example—the problem is that many don't acknowledge that they don't know and try to tell you what to do. They don't want to hear, and think they know it all."*
> *—Participant*

- **Promote an open, accepting attitude.** Take a welcoming, warm, accepting, non-judgmental, compassionate and open stance. *(Strength-based approaches that promote hope; Person-first [culturally competent] approaches)*

- **Foster openness and humility.** Ensure that staff and volunteers are confident about their own knowledge but also open to learning how much they do not know and recognizing the people they serve as some of their best teachers. *(Person- and family-directed approaches; Strength-based approaches that promote hope; Person-first [culturally competent] approaches)*

- **Foster respectful listening.** Listen actively and attentively to each person and appreciate the individual's and the family's perception and understanding of their current

> *"Kids open up to care: try to get to know me, connect with me on a personal level, get to understand my point of view. Ask me relaxed questions; don't drill me. I had one therapist who hammered me with questions. I didn't tell him anything. Then I had another therapist who asked me the same questions ... but because of her way with me, I told her a lot of things; she made me feel like talking to her."*
> *—Youth*

challenges. Learn more about all of the people involved in or around the conditions they seek to address. *(Person- and family-directed approaches; Person-first [culturally competent] approaches)*

- **Respect and address elements of culture.** Ensure that outreach and intake services are truly culturally competent and that staff and volunteers have the humility to learn about culture from individuals and families. Ask people respectfully about their cultural heritage and ways in which their current challenges are viewed and addressed within their culture. *(Person-first [culturally competent] approaches)*

**Objective:** Use trauma-informed engagement strategies

**Potential Strategies:**

- **Promote trauma-informed intake interviews.** Use consistently respectful, patient, trauma-informed methods of intake

  - **Create safety and a sense of control within initial sessions,** through positive interactions with all staff (including reception staff) and volunteers and collaborative negotiation of conditions within sessions (e.g., where they sit, how far away others are sitting, what they discuss, how their privacy will be safeguarded). *(Trauma-informed approaches)*

  - **Use non-shaming ways of recognizing and eliciting information about ongoing unsafe conditions (e.g., family violence) and offering support and resources in safety planning.** *(Trauma-informed approaches)*

  - **Use terms that normalize post-trauma effects.** Use language that conveys the understanding that traumatic events and processes can happen in anyone's life and that post-trauma effects are normal and natural responses to these experiences. *(Strength-based approaches that promote hope; Trauma-informed approaches)*

- **Prevent harassment and coercion** by ensuring that policies, training, staff and employee actions, supervision and employee evaluation and correction processes maintain a clear distinction between assertive outreach and potential harassment or coercion, and correct any harassment or coercion immediately. *(Person- and family-directed approaches; Trauma-informed approaches)*

# Domain 1: Assertive Outreach and Initial Engagement

## Goal E: Provide Individualized Services to Identify and Address Barriers to Wellness

**Objective:** Ensure that all organizational barriers are recognized and addressed

**Potential Strategies:**

- **Identify and address barriers to engagement and participation.** Regularly review circumstances and practices that have kept individuals and families from engaging or remaining in treatment and other recovery support services. Institute changes in policy and practice to address those barriers. *(Person-first [culturally appropriate] approaches; Person- and family-directed approaches; Holistic approaches toward care)*

- **Look for barriers before discontinuing outreach.** Before concluding that an individual or family is not sufficiently motivated to receive services, actively look for signs that organizational or systemic barriers may be preventing engagement or participation. *(Person-first [culturally appropriate] approaches; Person- and family-directed approaches; Holistic approaches toward care)*

- **Use peers to help identify and lift barriers to wellness.** Empower peers to help individuals and families identify the challenges they might encounter in their ongoing efforts to sustain wellness and recovery. *(Person-first [culturally appropriate] approaches; Holistic approaches toward care; Peer culture, support and leadership)*

- **Provide screening, outreach and referral in participants' language.** Provide information, screening services, outreach, linkages and referrals in every language that is the first language of a significant percentage of the population to be served. When translation is necessary for the initial interview, use professional translators rather than relying on someone who has a personal relationship with the individual or family. *(Person-first [culturally competent] approaches)*

- **Address child care issues.** Make on-site child care available during appointments, or help participants find and arrange for child care. *(Holistic approaches toward care; Care for the needs and safety of children and adolescents)*

- **Address transportation obstacles.** Help participants plan access to public transportation and learn to navigate transportation systems. *(Holistic approaches toward care)*

**Objective:** Ensure that staff support individuals and families during transitions

**Potential Strategies:**

- **Provide interim services for people on waiting lists.** When a waiting list is the only option, offer less intensive interim services (e.g., peer-based support services) to address immediate needs and keep people engaged. *(Person-first [culturally appropriate] approaches; Holistic approaches toward care)*

- **Provide assertive linkage during transitions.** Use peer-based recovery support staff and volunteers (e.g., peer specialists, recovery/wellness coaches) to provide assertive linkage and support to individuals making the transition from detoxification, inpatient, residential and Crisis Response Center services to ongoing treatment and support services. *(Person-first [culturally appropriate] approaches; Holistic approaches toward care; Peer culture, support and leadership)*

- **Offer reminders in early engagement.** During the early engagement process, give individuals (particularly youth) the option to receive appointment reminders through telephone prompts or text messages, to increase rates of participation. *(Person-first [culturally appropriate] approaches; Holistic approaches toward care; Care for the needs and safety of children and adolescents)*

# Domain 1: Assertive Outreach and Initial Engagement

## Goal F: Achieve Successful Outcomes through Empirically Informed Approaches

**Objective:** Use empirically informed approaches to identify the need for services in earlier stages of problem development

Potential Strategies:

- **Identify and use empirically supported brief screening instruments** for a variety of challenges (e.g., substance use disorders, depression, posttraumatic stress disorder and other anxiety disorders). *(Holistic approaches toward care)*

- **Provide assertive referrals** to appropriate treatment modalities, levels of care and other recovery support services. Referral techniques might include calling the appropriate services in the presence of the individual or family during the intervention session, explaining the intake process, using peer support to accompany people to initial appointments and making follow-up calls to identify any barriers to services. *(Holistic approaches toward care)*

**Objective:** Facilitate service entry through empirically supported approaches

Potential Strategies:

- **Use empirically supported process-improvement tools.** Implement empirically  supported process-improvement tools such as those in the NIATx model, to reduce waiting lists and to remove obstacles for the many individuals and families who will seek help only in a crisis and will not follow through with care if it has been delayed. *(Person-first [culturally appropriate] approaches; Holistic approaches toward care)*

**Objective:** Identify and use empirically supported approaches to initial engagement

Potential Strategies:

- **Offer pre-treatment services.** Along with regular treatment services, make pre-treatment services available to those who are not ready to commit to services, or are on waiting lists. *(Person-first [culturally appropriate] approaches; Holistic approaches toward care)*

> "Focus on 'readiness to change' and engagement… blame is [often] placed on the family or person in recovery, rather than looking at how we engaged them and tried to build their motivation."
> *—Provider*

- **Utilize empirically supported clinical practices.** Design intake and engagement strategies so that, from the earliest interactions, staff use empirically supported practices such as motivational interviewing, contingency management and cognitive behavioral techniques (Stitzer & Petry, 2006). *(Person-first [culturally appropriate] approaches; Holistic approaches toward care)*

# Domain 1: Assertive Outreach and Initial Engagement

## Goal G: Promote Recovery and Resilience through Evaluation and Quality Improvement

**Objective:** Monitor the success of outreach and engagement efforts

**Potential Strategies:**

- **Monitor the success of community-based screening processes.** Document the success of, and challenges in, screening and brief intervention efforts in primary care settings, schools, community organizations, etc. Institute process-improvement measures as appropriate. *(Community inclusion, partnership and collaboration)*

- **Monitor indicators of initial engagement** (e.g., "no shows," the frequency with which people come back for return appointments), both by service unit/type and by individual staff member, and use this information in employee evaluation and process-improvement measures. *(Person-first [culturally appropriate] approaches)*

- **Assess the existence of any disparities in accessing care.** Disaggregate data by race, ethnicity and gender to evaluate the extent to which the populations represented in your community are accessing your services. *(Person-first [culturally appropriate] approaches)*

**Objective:** Use evaluation and quality improvement processes to ensure safe and effective outreach to individuals, families and allies

**Potential Strategies:**

- **Document steps to engage families and allies.** Create formal documentation of all steps taken to engage families and allies. Include a review of this documentation in each quality assurance or quality improvement effort, discuss the results with staff involved and implement any improvements needed (Family Resource Network, 2010). *(Family inclusion and leadership)*

- **Include individuals and family members in evaluation.** Design and implement participatory evaluation strategies to include both individuals and family members.

# Section III: Strategies in the Four Domains

# Domain 2: Screening, Assessment, Service Planning and Service Delivery

# Domain Overview

Optimize the effectiveness of service delivery.

- Focus services on recovery initiation and long-term recovery maintenance
- Utilize evidence-based and other empirically supported treatment approaches to increase the effectiveness of services
- Increase the participation and engagement of the individual, the family and other supporters in the entire service delivery process
- Individualize treatment based on factors known to have an effect on service outcomes (e.g. spirituality, culture, gender, strengths, experience of trauma, co-occurring conditions)
- Promote and enhance resilience and protective factors in children and families

# Section III: Strategies in the Four Domains

# Domain 2: Screening, Assessment, Service Planning and Service Delivery

## Background and Rationale

The understanding and management of behavioral health conditions has advanced dramatically in recent years, prompting fundamental changes in the areas of screening, assessment, service planning and service delivery. Foundational principles that guide this transformative process include self-determination, focus on quality of life, active participation and empowerment, promotion of and high expectations for recovery and resilience, community access and inclusion, a diverse and flexible array of service and support options, full access to information and responsible risk-taking and growth (DBH/MRS, 2006).

System transformation has been informed by an understanding that co-occurring mental health and substance-related challenges, combined with the ravages of poverty, the historical and present-day impact of trauma and a host of physical health issues, are hard realities for most of those who seek our services. A strength-based approach to screening, assessment, service planning and service delivery must acknowledge and address these challenges in order to identify and design the individual, system and community supports that can ignite and sustain resilience and recovery.

Central to this approach is the need and determination to focus on recovery capital rather than deficits, and to identify and incorporate recovery capital into screening, assessment, service planning and service delivery. Recovery capital includes all the internal and external resources mobilized to initiate and sustain long-term recovery (White & Cloud, 1998). It is through the identification and mobilization of recovery capital that staff, family members, allies and peers can help people make effective use of their own internal and external resources in overcoming their current challenges.

In a recovery- and resilience-oriented organization or system, assessment is conducted in a strength-based fashion, giving priority to the identification of assets, interests and resources as well as difficulties. A person-first assessment is based on strengths and embraces the principles of cultural competence, weaving clinical knowledge and its application within the cultural context of the individual and family seeking services and the community in which they live.

Service planning is also based on strengths in the individual, family, community and culture. The individual authors his or her service plan, resulting in an individualized, multidisciplinary plan developed in partnership with all provider staff involved in service delivery, family members and other allies. The plan is connected to the enhancement of the participant's life in the community.

At its core, person-directed care planning affirms and actively supports an individual's hopes and dreams, while mobilizing the requisite psychiatric, medical, social, vocational, educational and community-based supports that will inspire action, create momentum and acknowledge progress in the recovery journey (DBH/MRS, 2006). Service delivery begins with, and continues to include, ongoing assessment and planning efforts. The service plan becomes a "living document" that grows and changes as the individual and family, and their needs and capabilities, grow and change.

Many of the clinical practices that have developed in traditional models are consistent with recovery- and resilience-driven approaches. However, clinicians need to take extra care to structure and deliver these services within a framework that is person and family centered, collaborative and rooted in the community in which the individual lives.

For example, behavioral health organizations use multiple approaches to keep people engaged, and organizations employ a number of targeted effectiveness measures and strategies for overcoming barriers to care.

Service teams are inclusive and collaborative, with participants in key decision-making roles and appropriate family members, allies and peers playing important support roles.

Clinical services work hand-in-hand with peer- and community-based recovery support services. As often as possible, services are located in the community and coordinated with community-based sources of support.

This transformation in the areas of screening, assessment, service planning and service delivery also sets the stage for transformation of larger systems of care, provider organizations, staff, families, the recovery community and their allies, by modeling and promoting a strength-based approach in which every person involved has an important role to play in individual, family and community growth and achievement. The recognition of individual resilience factors, the commitment to self-determination and the willingness to shift the focus toward community engagement form both the conceptual bedrock of this transformation process and the engine of change for people receiving services.

Recovery-driven screening, assessment, service planning and service delivery processes:

- energize the growth of individual, family and community resilience factors;
- support self-determination; and
- enhance access to meaningful community life for all participants.

All individuals and family members deserve to have confidence in a process that values their input and incorporates it into plans and strategies for success.

# Domain 2: Screening, Assessment, Service Planning and Service Delivery

## Goal A: Provide Integrated Services

**Objective:** Develop relationships with primary care providers to promote integrated services

Potential Strategies:

- **Expand service-delivery partnerships with primary care providers** by increasing their awareness of the types of services you offer, demonstrating the value of your services and exploring strategies for service integration and bi-directional co-location. Identify opportunities to become integrated partners in developing person- centered health care homes and Accountable Care Organizations. *(Community inclusion, partnership and collaboration)*

- **Explore new options for cross training.** Consider hosting multidisciplinary symposia with representatives of primary care, behavioral health, peer and community based recovery support services; facilitate discussion forums and in-service training sessions (e.g., brown-bag lunch discussions, grand rounds presentations) to promote partnerships. *(Community inclusion, partnership and collaboration)*

- **Address primary health care needs and perceptions.** Structure assessment and service planning and delivery processes (both clinical and non-clinical recovery supports) to attend carefully to the individual's primary health care needs and experience of overall health (physical, behavioral and the intersection of the two). *(Holistic approaches toward care)*

**Objective:** Use collaborative relationships with a variety of community-based service providers and supports to strengthen recovery and resilience

Potential Strategies:

- **Form partnerships that will foster participants' strengths.** Identify agencies, organizations and institutions that provide services to help participants develop their strengths and work toward their goals. These might include community colleges, vocational training and assistance organizations, recovery community business enterprises, community-based sources of training in self-defense, etc. *(Community partnership and collaboration; Strength-based approaches that promote hope)*

- **Engage the faith-based and secular communities.** Create formal and informal mechanisms for forging relationships with a variety of faith-based and secular communities and services. Include discussion that will educate each entity on the approaches and activities of the other, and guidelines for safe and appropriate referral *(Holistic approaches toward care; Community partnership and collaboration)*

# Domain 2: Screening, Assessment, Service Planning and Service Delivery

## Goal B: Create an Atmosphere that Promotes Strength, Recovery and Resilience

**Objective:** Promote hope in all screening, assessment, service planning and delivery processes

Potential Strategies:

- **Assess the organizational climate and address any recurring staff concerns.** Understand that promoting hope is a parallel process and that staff will be better positioned to promote hope in the individuals and families they serve when they feel positive about their work environment and valued for their contributions (*Strength-based approaches that promote hope)*

- **Create an atmosphere of trust and mutual learning.** Minimize the presence of and dependence on forms and protocols in sessions. *(Strength-based approaches that promote hope)*

- **Relate to the person first.** In getting to know individuals and families, view them as people first and foremost, with such issues as diagnoses, presenting problems and psychosocial history playing important but secondary roles. *(Strength-based approaches that promote hope; Person-first [culturally competent] approaches)*

**Objective:** Foster environments that nourish and support children and families

Potential Strategies:

- **Promote multi-level nurturing environments for children.** Employ multiple means of creating nurturing environments for children, including the following:

  - **Promote positive family rituals and interactions** through family sessions, exploration of existing patterns within the family and referral to family centered activities in the community. *(Family inclusion and leadership)*

  - **Explore and strengthen coping skills that come naturally** to children through a variety of activities (e.g., play, social activities, extracurricular activities). *(Care for the needs and safety of children and adolescents)*

  - **Find community-based sources of support,** such as support groups or through school or community programs (Edelsohn & Forman, 2010). *(Care for the needs and safety of children and adolescents)*

- **Create family-friendly organizations.** Develop family-friendly waiting rooms with books and toys for children, printed information about family education and support groups, etc. Include family members and key allies as board members and/or in policy and planning decisions. *(Family inclusion and leadership; Care for the needs and safety of children and adolescents)*

# Domain 2: Screening, Assessment, Service Planning and Service Delivery

## Goal C: Develop Inclusive, Collaborative Service Teams and Processes

**Objective:** Make peer support staff an integral part of service teams

**Potential Strategies:**

- **Ensure that participants have access to peer support.** Within the organization ensure that participants have access to both formal (paid) and informal (volunteer) peer support. *(Strength-based approaches that promote hope; Peer culture, support and leadership)*

- **Create a family peer support role** using paid staff who focus on engaging families in services, helping staff identify families' basic needs and monitoring the fulfillment of those needs. *(Family inclusion and leadership; Peer culture, support and leadership)*

- **Identify potential peer leaders.** Use the information collected in assessment and planning processes (e.g., individual strengths, talents, resilience factors, recovery capital) to help identify new peer leaders. *(Peer culture, support and leadership)*

- **Promote and develop peer leaders.** Identify and cultivate opportunities for individuals to develop and use their leadership skills. *(Peer culture, support and leadership)*

  - **Develop peer leadership councils or advisory councils that include peers and families,** and give these councils real power in affecting program development, evaluation and improvement. *(Peer culture, support and leadership; Family inclusion and leadership)*

> *"We could help, if someone gave us a chance." "Giving back makes you feel better..... gives you hope for the future." "We could help to lead peer support groups." "We could help new people in recovery find their way." "We could help people find resources and good places to go that we have found."*
> —People in Recovery in Philadelphia

**Objective:** Implement policies that promote true partnership in service teams

**Potential Strategies:**

- **Build effective multidisciplinary teams** that blend the knowledge and experience of all team members (e.g., psychiatrists, psychologists, social workers, counselors, peers, family members, primary care providers, other cross-system partners) and employ these resources in service of the participant's recovery. *(Strength-based approaches that promote hope; Person- and family-directed approaches)*

- **Create and sustain an organization-wide partnership/consultation model.** Shift the service delivery philosophy from an expert model to a partnership/consultation approach. Ensure that individuals and families are involved and supported in key decision-making processes regarding their services (Mayor's Blue Ribbon Commission, 2007, Recommendation 2:1). *(Person- and family-directed approaches; Strength-based approaches that promote hope)*

- **Promote shared decision-making** in all service planning and delivery processes. Set up structures, procedures and instructions that:

  - **Honor the expertise and autonomy of each individual in determining his or her own needs; values; and preferences for treatment, rehabilitation and other recovery supports** *(Person- and family-directed approaches; Strength-based approaches that promote hope; Family inclusion and leadership)*

  - **Honor the expertise that professionals bring to the service team.** Ensure that professionals understand that their role is no less important than those of other members of the service team, or that their skills are valued less highly. Instead, they work as partners alongside the individuals and families they serve, the peer support providers and other service team members *(Peer culture, support and leadership; Partnership and transparency)*

  - **Use the expertise and support of allies and peers who assist them on the service team.** *(Person- and family-directed approaches; Strength-based approaches that promote hope; Peer culture, support and leadership)*

  - **Promote participant choice in the planning process itself.** Establish procedures for plan development that allow the participant to choose, not only the services included in the plan, but also the method of plan development and management that gives him or her the greatest ownership of the plan (e.g., writing it him/herself, keeping it in his or her possession). *(Person- and family-directed approaches; Strength-based approaches that promote hope)*

- **Invite families and allies to participate as partners.** Acknowledge that families and allies have their own expertise and intimate knowledge of the individual, and encourage everyone to ask questions, review their options and voice possible disagreements as members of the multidisciplinary team. Promote empowerment of parents as equal experts on behalf of their children. Assure families and allies that neither they nor the participant will suffer repercussions as a result of their questioning or disagreeing with providers. *(Person- and family-directed approaches; Family inclusion and leadership)*

- **Tailor family influence to participants' ages and adults' choices.** In developing approaches toward assessment, service planning and service delivery, respect the difference between the influence of family and allies on children/adolescents and their influence on adults. The central role of family in service planning for children is without question. However, for adults, the individual determines the role of family and allies in service planning. *(Person- and family-directed approaches; Family inclusion and leadership; Care for the needs and safety of children and adolescents)*

# Domain 2: Screening, Assessment, Service Planning and Service Delivery

## Goal D: Provide Services, Training and Supervision that Promote Recovery and Resilience

**Objective:** Ensure that staff use recovery-oriented interviewing skills in order to conduct effective assessments

**Potential Strategies:**

- **Focus on building relationships during assessments.** Establish an open, trusting relationship, including an accepting and non-judgmental attitude, a willingness to provide complete information about assessment and diagnostic procedures, a willingness to answer the individual's and the family's questions and an ability to be open to and understanding of their needs and concerns. *(Strength-based approaches that promote hope; Person- and family-directed approaches; Person-first [culturally competent] approaches)*

- **Record information in the participant's terms.** During assessment and service planning, record the individual's responses in terms he or she would use, recognize and understand. This helps to ensure that the assessment remains narrative based and person directed. When technical language is necessary, translate it appropriately and present it in a person-first manner. *(Person-first [culturally competent] approaches)*

> *"I always tell my students that the first time you see someone (and all the times after that) is a chance for healing. They come to you with challenges and often with a history of trauma, and they wait to see if you are going to reject them. These are people who are used to being overlooked, ignored and hurt, but if you do it, they won't trust you, won't open up and won't come back."*
> —Seasoned Provider

- **View assessments as "living documents"** that continue to be explored and updated throughout treatment and recovery support processes, rather than limiting them to an intake function. *(Person- and family-directed approaches; Person-first [culturally competent] approaches)*

- **Promote strength-based language for children.** Adopt assessment and service-planning practices that will help children develop and use strength-based language in speaking about their challenges, rather than using the labels that others may have applied to them in the past. *(Strength-based approaches that promote hope; Care for the needs and safety of children and adolescents)*

**Objective:** Explore the full range of experience, including strengths and challenges

**Potential Strategies:**

- **Use comprehensive assessment for children and adolescents.** Structure assessment and service-planning processes for children and adolescents that address all of the following: cognitive and school functioning; peer relations; family relationships; physical development and medical history; emotional development, temperament and mental state; development of conscience and values; interests, hobbies, talents, avocations and strengths; prior psychiatric treatment history; all substance-related history and current use; children's and adolescents' own aspirations; problem-solving capability and strategies used in the past; and understanding of individual and family resilience *(Care for the needs and safety of children and adolescents; Holistic approaches toward care)*

- **Assess and address developmental challenges within a recovery framework.** Establish procedures that allow staff to understand and address the developmental challenges of children, adolescents, families and allies within a recovery and resilience framework. Combine the use of standardized instruments for measuring strengths and challenges of children and adolescents with a recovery/resilience approach to engagement. *(Strength-based approaches that promote hope; Care for the needs and safety of children and adolescents)*

- **Use open and creative methods of finding and focusing on strengths:**
  - **Use families and allies to help assess individuals' strengths.** Develop strength-based assessments through in-depth discussion with the individual and attempts to solicit collateral information about strengths from the individual's family and natural supports. (Family inclusion and leadership; Strength-based approaches that *promote hope)*
  - **Use peers to help assess recovery capital.** Use peer specialists to help assess each individual's protective factors, resilience factors and recovery capital (on individual, family and community levels). (Peer culture, support and leadership; Strength-based approaches *that promote hope)*
  - **Find and acknowledge the strengths within perceived deficits.** Help participants and families understand that their challenging characteristics are often the extreme expression of significant strengths within them (e.g., anger as the extreme of passion, "people-pleasing" as the extreme of consideration or diplomacy). Look at ways in which supposed deficits might be considered assets in the participant's culture, family or community. *(Strength-based approaches that promote hope;*

*Person-first [culturally competent] approaches)*

- **Find strengths even in traumatic histories.** Adopt procedures and train staff to identify the strengths, capabilities, capacities, talents, problem-solving abilities, etc. of those who have lived with traumatic experiences, and to help the individual use these strengths to address current challenges in a safe and hopeful environment. *(Trauma-informed approaches; Strength-based approaches that promote hope)*

- **Gain a broad view of children's and adolescents' strengths.** During evaluation interviews and the initial data-gathering phase, elicit areas of strength, interests and achievements; note participation in clubs, sports and faith-based activities; and assess positive attachments and ways in which past stressors have been successfully negotiated. (Examples of strength-based assessment strategies can be found in Appendix E) *(Care for the needs and safety of children and adolescents; Holistic approaches toward care; Strength-based approaches that promote hope)*

- **Include strengths in family assessments.** In family assessments, include family and individual member strengths, talents and experience; family and individual aspirations, hopes and dreams; the family's and the individual's previous success in addressing behavioral health challenges within the family; and an exploration of family resilience factors that might be mobilized to address current challenges *(Family inclusion and leadership; Strength-based approaches that promote hope)*

- **Assess the quality of family connections.** Assess the individual's current involvement in and connection with family and allies and the extent to which people communicate about their hopes and dreams for change and improvement. Explore ways in which family members and allies have been helpful or harmful in the past and any challenges that might have arisen in these relationships. *(Family inclusion and leadership)*

- **Assess social foundations for recovery.** Assess (and understand in the person's language) the presence, degree and quality of social connections, the individual's sense of belonging and his or her participation in family and community activities. Discuss these as essential foundations for advancing recovery and resilience. *(Strength-based approaches that promote hope)*

  - **Identify and use family resources.** Explore participants' family, kinship and natural support networks to identify resources that they believe might be helpful in supporting and maintaining their own wellness. Work collaboratively with participants to educate family members and other important allies in ways of identifying participants' characteristic signs that they might need re-intervention. *(Family inclusion and leadership; Person- and family-directed approaches)*

- **Assess the availability of peer support.** Consult assessments for the presence (or absence) of supportive peers, keeping in mind that, while peer groups serve different functions at different stages across the life span, information about their presence (or absence) and helpfulness (or potential for injury) is a critical element in understanding the community support available to children, youth and adults. *(Peer culture, support and leadership)*

- **Assess, acknowledge and harness cultural strengths.** Train staff to recognize the traditional and contemporary cultural elements that add to participants' and families' strength, resilience and recovery capital, and to help participants and families discover, appreciate and tap into these strengths. *(Person-first [culturally competent] approaches)*

- In the assessment process, reflect positive skills and strengths back to the individual, using developmentally appropriate language. *(Recovery-oriented clinical and organizational services)*

**Objective:** Extend beyond traditional assessment of challenges and needs

**Potential Strategies:**

- **Explore cultural approaches to addressing challenges.** With each challenge identified, ask people about their cultural heritage and ways in which these challenges are viewed and addressed within their culture. *(Person-first [culturally competent] approaches)*

- **Explore the ways in which cultural identity might affect the identified challenge.** Ask people about the ways in which they identify themselves culturally, and the ways in which their cultural identity and experience might affect their challenges and coping. For example, explore the impact of discrimination, racism, homophobia and sexism on current challenges. *(Person-first [culturally competent] approaches)*

- **Assess the need for general wellness approaches.** Design the assessment process to include exploration of the extent to which the individual might benefit from daily wellness approaches such as WRAP (Wellness Recovery Action Planning) and training in self-management strategies for coping with symptoms. *(Holistic approaches toward care)*

- **Include medication support in ongoing assessment.** Structure the ongoing assessment process to include collaboration and consultation in medication management.

  - **Include all psychiatric and non-psychiatric medical**

**professionals prescribing** either psychotropic or non-psychotropic medications. *(Cross-system partnership, coordination and collaboration; Person- and family-directed approaches; Holistic approaches toward care)*

- **Involve the entire team (including individuals, family members and allies)** in the assessment of the efficacy of medications; the impact of side effects; and interactions among pharmacotherapy, other treatment modalities and strength-based activities. *(Person- and family-directed approaches; Holistic approaches toward care)*

- Assess the need for parenting support and education:

  - **Assess the need for parenting education and support** for individuals who are or are at risk of abusing or neglecting their children *(Trauma-informed approaches; Care for the needs and safety of children; Family inclusion and leadership)*

  - **Provide comprehensive training for this aspect of assessment,** including information about ways in which parents who are also experiencing the effects of abuse in their own lives may have trouble taking in new information and learning new skills in this area until the impact of their own trauma is addressed. *(Trauma-informed approaches)*

  - **Intervene in any direct danger to children's safety,** as appropriate. Use partnerships with Child Protective Services to promote the safety and well being of participants/families and their children. *(Trauma-informed approaches; Care for the needs and safety of children)*

  - **Support parents in their efforts at family reunification.** When it is safe and appropriate, use recovery-oriented strategies to assist parents in maintaining or regaining custody of their children from Child Protective Services. (*Care for the needs and safety of children)*

**Objective:** Create resilience and recovery-oriented planning processes

**Potential Strategies:**

- **Link recovery-oriented assessment and service plans.** Use the assessment of the individual's and family's hopes, strengths, interests and goals to drive the development of a comprehensive service plan. *(Person- and family-directed approaches; Partnership and multidisciplinary service plans)*

- **Elicit participants' preferences and interests** as a positive foundation for effective service planning, service delivery and the development of a more gratifying life in the community. This is particularly important for program participants who have not focused on their individual hopes and dreams in previous health care service relationships. *(Person- and family-directed approaches; Strength-based approaches that promote hope; Person-first [culturally competent] approaches)*

- **Elicit incremental, concrete goals and tasks** that are achievable within a short period of time (a rapid time cycle) and within normal, everyday community settings. This will support the development of a "success culture" within the relationship among the individual, staff, family and allies. *(Strength-based approaches that promote hope)*

- **Create a menu of services and supports** from which participants, families and allies can choose to support the recovery and resilience of all. *(Strength-based approaches that promote hope; Holistic approaches toward care; Person- and family-directed approaches)*

- **Engage peers in participants' service planning** and wellness and recovery planning processes.
  - **Use the natural partnerships that develop** both within and outside the formal program to support the individual's ability to take new risks toward achieving recovery tasks and goals. *(Peer culture, support and leadership)*
  - **Actively foster intentional "buddy" partnerships** among peers that can initiate and sustain social support and allow partners to help one another toward achievable goals and tasks in their service plans. *(Peer culture, support and leadership)*

**Objective:** Create comprehensive, holistic service plans

**Potential Strategies:**

- **Create holistic service plans**, including the following:
  - **Reflect a community focus.** Frame the impact of and solutions to challenges within the context of the individual's and the family's desire to build, rebuild, or preserve a meaningful life in the community. *(Community inclusion, partnership and collaboration)*
  - **Ensure that the service plan identifies a wide range** of professional services, natural supports and alternative strategies to bolster the individual's and the family's wellness, with particular emphasis on those that have been helpful to others with similar struggles. Combine information about medications and other clinical treatments with information about the range of services and supports available (e.g., mutual-aid groups and activities, peer support, exercise, nutrition, daily maintenance activities, spiritual practices and affiliations, homeopathic and naturopathic remedies). *(Holistic approaches toward care)*

**Objective:** Integrate the full range of services that support recovery into the plan

**Potential Strategies:**

- **Include wellness approaches in service plans.** If indicated in the assessment, include the use of daily wellness approaches such as WRAP (Wellness Recovery Action Planning) and training in self-management strategies for coping with symptoms. *(Strength-based approaches that promote hope; Holistic approaches toward care)*

- **Include primary care in service plans.** Structure the service plan to attend carefully to the individual's experience of physical health and the primary health care system. *(Holistic approaches toward care)*

- **Include community support groups and peer support in service plans.** Include in the service plan support services in group modalities that take place in natural settings such as communities, schools, etc. These services might include, for example, life skills groups, psychoeducational groups, family support groups and adolescent peer groups. Take advantage of the natural peer support that develops. *(Person- and family-directed approaches; Peer culture, support and leadership)*

> *"Tell me something about yourself. If I know anything about you beyond what degrees you have, it helps me to open up...But don't tell me too much about yourself. I had a therapist who told me all her trouble. That wasn't what I was there for."*
> —Person in Recovery

**Objective:** **Establish boundaries and safety measures for recovery and resilience-oriented care**

**Potential Strategies:**

- **Prepare staff for appropriate self-disclosure.** Ensure that staff understand the value of self-disclosure when it is appropriate and appreciate the common humanity that ties us all together, regardless of illness, disability or any other consideration. However, prepare staff to ensure that their own self-disclosure is not a burden to the participant, and to distinguish clearly between disclosure for the participant's sake and disclosure that fulfills their own needs. *(Strength-based approaches that promote hope; Trauma-informed approaches)*

- **Facilitate changes in service providers.** Create a process through which people can safely and smoothly change service providers within the agency if they are not satisfied or comfortable, and make this procedure well known and easily accessible. Give them the option to initiate this process through a neutral third party if they are feeling intimidated. *(Person- and family-directed approaches; Person-first [culturally competent] approaches; Trauma-informed approaches)*

**Objective:** Create and offer peer support options for individuals and families

Potential Strategies:

- **Create peer groups.** Give participants options for peer-led support groups, both on site and in the community. Where appropriate and feasible, create culture-specific (e.g., age, gender, language, ethnicity) groups. *(Peer culture, support and leadership)*
- **Use peers to address the needs of children of troubled families.** Create safe peer groups or link with other peer support for pre-teens or adolescents in families in which substance use, mental illness or other challenges are present (e.g., families facing homelessness or foreclosure, families with a parent or sibling receiving services). *(Care for the needs and safety of children and adolescents; Peer culture, support and leadership)*

**Objective:** Offer a range of services to families

Potential Strategies:

- **Address family strengths, needs and challenges in care:** Use a multidimensional approach in designing and delivering family-specific services, education and support. *(Family inclusion and leadership)*
- **Provide support for families and other allies.** Through assessment, treatment and support, offer ongoing peer support and educational resources or referrals to families and other involved allies. Create paid or volunteer family support roles. *(Family inclusion and leadership; Strength-based approaches that promote hope)*
- **Offer family therapy** to individuals and families who would like this service. Provide assertive referrals to any specialized family services that are beyond the organization's expertise. *(Family inclusion and leadership)*
- **Continue to engage families through telephone strategies** that decrease both initial no-show rates and early service termination. *(Family inclusion and leadership)*

**Objective:** Align training content and processes to support recovery and resilience-oriented screening, assessment, service planning and service delivery

Potential Strategies:

- **Provide training for staff on ways of promoting shared decision making.** Staff are often concerned about how to support individuals and families if they do not agree with their decisions or do not think the decisions are in their best interest. Staff will need assistance in understanding that shared decision making does not mean that staff have no input, no role and no influence. Instead, rather than dictating the decisions or directions, they work collaboratively to assist people in thinking through the advantages and disadvantages associated with specific decisions. When they have concerns, they express and document those concerns, and work with participants to explore other alternatives. However, they also understand that, unless there are safety issues, people ultimately have the power to make decisions about their lives. Instead of requiring less involvement on the part of providers, this type of interaction requires *greater* clinical sophistication, and staff may benefit from case studies, role-playing and other interactive training techniques.

- **Train staff to assess the quality of the therapeutic alliance** throughout the care process, by soliciting and using feedback from individuals and families on the quality of the partnership they have formed and the care they are receiving. *(Strength-based approaches that promote hope; Person- and family-directed approaches)*

- **Educate all staff on the power of language.** Train staff to recognize and avoid the subtle messages of dismissal, disregard and disrespect that professional language can convey toward people with psychiatric diagnoses, people with addiction and their loved ones. Increase staff's use of language that is empowering and avoids eliciting pity or sympathy, to avoid casting people with disabilities in a passive "victim" role and reinforcing negative stereotypes. *(Person-first [culturally competent] approaches)*

- **Train staff to engage in respectful listening.** Development of true partnership requires that staff listen attentively to each individual and appreciate the individual's and the family's perception and understanding of their current challenges. Train staff to ask questions and listen actively to the individual's and/or family's responses, in order to learn more about all of the factors involved with the conditions they seek to address. *(Person-first [culturally competent] approaches; Person- and family-directed approaches)*

- **Train staff to respect exceptions to "person-first" language** that are preferred by some individuals in recovery (e.g., the utility of terms such as "alcoholic" or "addict" for some individuals with substance use disorders, particularly those who work the 12 Steps). When in doubt, ask the individual what terminology he or she prefers. Also be aware that people may refer to themselves one way within their mutual aid groups (e.g., AA members referring to themselves as *alcoholics* or *drunks* in meetings or in informal communication with one another) but use other language outside that culture. *(Person-first [culturally competent] approaches)*

- **Train staff on person-first, culturally responsive processes.** Through guidelines and staff training, ensure that all screening, assessment, planning and service delivery processes, formats and practices are person-first, culturally sensitive, culturally responsive and personally affirming to individuals within the cultural context/ group of the program. Ensure that all staff possess knowledge of the variety of cultures represented in the individuals they serve, their neighborhood and the community, and the ability to work in partnership within these cultures (refer to Appendix F for areas of inquiry to be addressed in conducting person-first assessments). *(Person-first [culturally competent] approaches)*

- **Prepare staff for effective work with children, youth and families who are involved with other systems.** Through training, supervision, mentorship and support, help staff learn to work effectively with partners in other systems without violating the trust of the individuals and families they serve. This may be critical to addressing the holistic needs of the children, youth and families they will encounter. *(Care for the needs and safety of children and adolescents)*

- **Prepare staff to enlist faith and spirituality.** Train staff in the importance of faith and spirituality, in its many expressions and in the engagement of many individuals and their families and communities. Create and use formal and informal structures for forging relationships with faith-based communities and services. Ensure that staff elicit and respect participants' and families' own choices and belief systems in choosing faith-based resources. *(Holistic approaches toward care; Person-first [culturally competent] approaches)*

- **Normalize post-trauma effects.** Train staff to convey the understanding that post-trauma effects are normal and natural responses to life experiences. *(Trauma-informed approaches)*

- **Train staff in recovery and resilience-based assessment.** Train staff to create a comfortable rapport and to conduct ongoing, comprehensive, strength-based, developmentally appropriate, trauma-informed and person-first assessments that take into account the individual's life context and ongoing goals and aspirations, as well as his or her presenting problems. Train practitioners to elicit and listen actively to stories, rather than follow a pre-determined checklist of symptoms and deficits. *(Strength-based approaches that promote hope; Person-first [culturally competent] approaches)*

- **Promote staff and volunteer self-care through training, supervision, mentorship and support.** Train, encourage and support staff and volunteers in the use of appropriate measures for self-care in working with people whose challenges are complex and whose stories hold much pain. This is particularly important with staff and volunteers who have their own histories of trauma, mental health issues and/or addiction. *(Trauma-informed approaches)*

- **Train staff to focus on participants' own priorities.** Train staff to look for, recognize and address individuals' and families' own priorities, concerns, goals and aspirations and to see the priorities dictated by their own training within the context of participants' priorities. Increase staff's ability to connect participants' goals to their interventions. *(Person- and family-directed approaches)*

- **Train staff in assessment of co-occurring challenges.** Train staff to identify and address or refer co-occurring behavioral health and primary care conditions, as well as the full range of challenges that can arise from the experience of poverty, or from involvement in the child welfare system or the criminal justice system. *(Person- and family-directed approaches)*

- **Train staff in trauma-informed assessment**, including the following:

  - **Address the central importance of generational, lived and current traumatic experience** (including traumatic experience in behavioral health settings) in the complexity and chronicity of individual and family mental health and substance use challenges. *(Trauma-informed approaches; Person-first [culturally competent] approaches)*

  - **Institute procedures (e.g., empirically supported tools and processes)** for accurately and sufficiently identifying the existence and degree of impact of trauma on the individual and family. *(Trauma-informed approaches; Person-first [culturally competent] approaches)*

  - **Make the assessment process respectful and patient,** using cues from the individual in determining the pacing of the interview. *(Trauma-informed approaches; Person- and family-directed approaches)*

  - **Include questions designed to respectfully elicit any existing trauma history.** *(Trauma-informed approaches)*

  - **Assess current safely levels** (e.g., at home, at school, in the community), and offer support and resources in safety planning. *(Trauma-informed approaches)*

# Domain 2: Screening, Assessment, Service Planning and Service Delivery

## Goal E: Provide Individualized Services to Identify and Address Barriers to Wellness

**Objective:** Use principles of recovery-oriented care to address barriers to wellness

Potential Strategies:

- **Provide stage-appropriate services.** Create a service structure that accommodates participants' stages of change. For example:
    - **Allow flexibility in outpatient care (e.g., doing away with arbitrary timelines).** *(Person- and family-directed approaches)*
    - **Provide low-intensity care for those who would not benefit from high-intensity treatment at the time.** *(Person- and family-directed approaches)*
    - **Provide a "fast track" for people who need only medication support.** *(Person- and family-directed approaches)*
    - **Design programs and services around people.** Build the structure and the content of the program around the individuals and families being served, rather than trying to fit people into predetermined program templates. (Person- and family-directed approaches)

> *"We always think that what people in recovery need is structure, so we developed a program that has the first group at 8.00 a.m., but we found that people in recovery who are homeless are not typically up at 8.00 a.m. So the program asked them, "What time should group be for you?"*
> *—Provider*

- **Reform administrative discharge policies.** In substance use treatment, revise administrative discharge policies so that individuals with addictions are not discharged or punished for resuming substance use (i.e., exhibiting symptoms of their medical conditions). Under these amended policies, individuals would be re-engaged (and, if necessary, re-stabilized within another level of care), and their care plans would be adjusted to meet their evolving needs. *(Person- and family-directed approaches)*

**Objective:** Address logistical barriers through greater flexibility

Potential Strategies:

- **Allow for choice in service logistics.** Provide flexible service hours that meet the needs of the community, and allow people to select times that accommodate their commitments. *(Person- and family-directed approaches; Community partnership and collaboration)*

- **Accommodate family members' scheduling needs and communication methods.** Involve family members in choosing times for team meetings. This is particularly critical for parents who may be juggling limited finances, care for young children, transportation issues, etc. Be flexible in efforts to accommodate their scheduling needs. Use any available communication technology (e-mail, phone conferences) that supports involvement, rather than requiring face-to-face meetings for every contact. *(Family inclusion and leadership; Person- and family-directed approaches)*

> *"We expect choice in our own lives, but we limit choice in the lives of the people that we serve."*
> —Philadelphia Provider

- **Deliver services in non-stigmatized community settings.** Address logistical barriers, participants' sense of shame and the gap between treatment and life by collaborating with community partners to deliver services in non-stigmatized community settings. For example, appropriate settings might include primary care centers, schools, youth recreational centers, community organizations and faith-based organizations (Alvarez et al., 2006). *(Strength-based approaches that promote hope; Community partnership and collaboration)*

- Address missed appointments through re-engagement. Use telephone calls, reminder notes, emails and text messaging to encourage re-engagement following missed appointments (Carroll, 1995). *(Person-first [culturally competent] services)*

**Objective:** Assess and address cultural barriers for each participant and family

**Potential Strategies:**

- **Monitor and address challenges related to culture.** Through supervision and quality-improvement methods, address any situations in which cultural differences might be affecting service access or satisfaction. Look for cultural barriers in location or treatment approaches and for cultural differences between participants and staff or volunteers, or between participants and roommates or other group members. Address issues of culture broadly defined, including ethnicity, gender, age, sexual orientation, religion, etc. *(Person-first [culturally competent] approaches)*

- **Remove language as a barrier.** Use appropriate resources that will assist in removing language as a barrier to access, or to the effectiveness or acceptability of ongoing services and supports. Include language barriers related, not only to culture of origin, but also to educational or developmental stages, particularly with children. *(Person-first [culturally competent] approaches)*

- **Institute and enforce clear anti-discrimination policies** that state clearly that racism, sexism, ageism, homophobia and other forms of discrimination are not acceptable, and provide guidance for interpretation and corrective measures (please see Appendix G for DBHIDS' policy on services to LGBTQI people). *(Person-first [culturally competent] approaches)*

> *"Don't use words I don't understand...I'm already scared; make me feel safe."*
> *—Youth*

- **Ensure that staff cultures reflect participant cultures.** At all levels of the organization, hire staff who reflect the racial/ethnic makeup of the largest cultural groups served, and ensure that individuals and families have access to staff or peers whom they perceive as having similar backgrounds, or at least as understanding their culture. *(Person-first [culturally competent] approaches)*

- **Employ young adults as adolescent peer support specialists.** In adolescent programs, create peer support specialist roles and employ adults who are closer in age to adolescents, to improve insight into their realities and increase adolescents' perception that staff understand their needs and concerns. *(Care for the needs and safety of children and adolescents; Person-first [culturally competent] approaches; Peer culture, support and leadership)*

- **Address gender and sexual orientation in matching staff to participants.** Safeguard individuals' well being by taking issues of gender, sexual orientation and homophobia into account and choosing combinations that will facilitate trust and minimize the risk of harassment. Also ensure that people receiving services have the opportunity to identify the best fit for themselves. *(Person-first [culturally competent] approaches)*

**Objective:** Assess and address barriers to participant safety in service settings

**Potential Strategies:**

- **Promote safe interactions in service delivery and service settings.** Establish and follow protocols for creating safety within treatment and recovery support settings, including protocols that:
    - **Monitor safety in relationships with staff, volunteers and other participants. Identify and address elements of danger or abuse as they arise. Ensure that participants understand that it is appropriate to report signs or feelings of danger, and that they are safe in doing so.** *(Trauma-informed approaches)*

- Improve individuals' ability to negotiate conditions within sessions, find alternatives to group processes that feel unsafe to them, and change providers or roommates if they feel unsafe in these relationships. *(Trauma-informed approaches; Person- and family-directed approaches)*
- Allow participants time to establish trusting relationships before they discuss traumatic material. *(Trauma-informed approaches)*
- Teach participants to modulate and manage their stress responses before they discuss traumatic material, to reduce the risk of hyperarousal and relapse and to prepare them for greater safety when traumatic memories do return. *(Trauma-informed approaches)*

- **Guard against staff reactions to vicarious traumatization.** Provide training, support and clinical supervision regarding the potential effects of secondary/ vicarious traumatization on staff, particularly on staff and volunteers with their own trauma histories. Educate supervisory and direct service staff on the connection between staff "burnout" and the risk of potentially harmful interactions or relationships with participants. *(Trauma-informed approaches)*

**Objective:** Address family and community barriers to care and recovery

**Potential Strategies:**

- **Identify and address situational stressors.** For participants with substance use disorders, identify individuals in their lives, locations in the home or community, activities in which they routinely engage and other circumstances that might raise the risk of urges and cravings or increase access to addictive substances. Work on plans that will make them aware of these risks and offer skills, strategies and support for coping with urges and making healthy choices. For individuals with mental health challenges, identify individuals, activities, circumstances or community settings that they believe have a negative impact on wellness, and identify plans to address or develop effective coping strategies. *(Person-first [culturally competent] approaches; Person- and family-directed approaches)*

# Domain 2: Screening, Assessment, Service Planning and Service Delivery

## Goal F: Achieve Successful Outcomes through Empirically Informed Approaches

**Objective:** Choose empirically informed approaches based on a thorough knowledge of principles and options

Potential Strategies:

- **Use empirically supported, comprehensive psychiatric assessment strategies for children and youth.** In adopting child, adolescent and family assessment strategies, study and follow the Practice Parameters for comprehensive psychiatric assessment of children and adolescents established by the American Academy of Child and Adolescent Psychiatry (available at http://www. aacap.org/galleries/PracticeParameters/Chiladol.pdf). Include a family assessment (available at http://www.aacap.org/galleries/ PracticeParameters/JAACAP_Family-2007.pdf) in the psychiatric evaluation of each child or adolescent: *"At a minimum, this means the clinician obtains family history from a caregiver and observes the interaction of the child with at least one caregiver. This indication is underscored by the fact that the family is the child's primary resource for healing and may be the child's primary source of distress. Its influence should never be underestimated. In some instances, it may be helpful to see the entire family together and in others it may be essential to do so. How the family interviews should be sequenced or combined varies with the case and clinical setting"* (AACAP, 2007, p. 922). *(Care for the needs and safety of children and adolescents; Family inclusion and leadership; Holistic approaches toward care)*

- **Use empirically supported approaches to intervention with families** (e.g., family psychoeducation), negotiating strategies and models of intervention (e.g., family consultation model) and confidentiality procedures (to lower the risk of inappropriate or inadequate communication with family members). *(Family inclusion and leadership; Strength-based approaches that promote hope; Person- and family-directed approaches)*

- **Examine and match available resources.** Before identifying specific strategies for screening, assessment, service planning and service delivery, examine the variety of empirically supported approaches that would be appropriate to participants' cultures and environments. Take into account the variety of cultural and community factors (e.g., culture, language, gender, age, sexual orientation, co-occurring disorders, socioeconomic status, educational level, criminal justice history). *(Person-first [culturally competent] approaches; Holistic approaches toward care)*

**Objective:** Choose treatment models that further a recovery orientation

**Potential Strategies:**

- **Use stages-of-change models in treatment.** Adopt empirically supported practices such as motivational interviewing, and ensure that services provided are consistent with people's stages of change. *(Strength-based approaches that promote hope)*
- **Use contingency management**, an empirically supported practice, to provide incentives for participation and to increase abstinence rates in addiction treatment. *(Strength-based approaches that promote hope)*

**Objective:** Follow the Philadelphia recommendations for services to children and youth

**Potential Strategies:**

- **Reflect core values in services for children and youth.** In designing screening, assessment and treatment services for children and adolescents, seek guidance from the Final Report (2007) of the Philadelphia Mayor's Blue Ribbon Commission (BRC) on Children's Behavioral Health. The BRC report articulated six big-picture goals and 22 recommendations, along with core values and guiding principles, to improve the social and emotional health of Philadelphia's children. A description of the BRC goals and recommendations is included in Appendix H. The core values are reflected in the following strategies:

  - Create plans that will **address children's needs in the most natural settings possible**, e.g., the home, the family, after-school centers, the community.
  - To the fullest extent possible, **allow families and children of all ages to participate** in all aspects of service planning and delivery.
  - Adopt evidence-informed practices that will **address the needs of children and youth.**
  - For children and families who have experienced childhood abuse and/or trauma, train staff to **understand their strengths and needs within a trauma-informed context.**
  - **Design planning processes for children and families** that will ensure integrated, coordinated care, regardless of the system or systems through which they receive it.
  - Ensure through the planning process that children have access

to an array of services that **address their physical, emotional, social and educational needs.**

- Include in the planning process services and supports that will **ensure a smooth transition from child to adult services.**

- Create service plans for children and their families that will **address their needs with high-quality services, regardless of service type or approach.**

- Ensure that service plans and the services themselves **emphasize the attainment of measurable, positive outcomes** (More information on these efforts in Philadelphia at http://www.dbhids.org/philadelphia-compact/).

**Objective:** Follow the Philadelphia practice guidelines for family inclusion

**Potential Strategies:**

- **Follow the "Standards for a Model Approach" guidelines.** In determining approaches toward family inclusion in assessment, service planning and service delivery, study and follow the practice guidelines outlined in *Standards for a Model Approach to Involving Consumer-Identified "Significant People" In Mental Health Treatment and Recovery Programs,* developed by the Philadelphia Family Resource Network in association with the Mental Health Association and the Philadelphia Department of Behavioral Health and Intellectual disAbility Services and the Family Involvement Practice Guidelines (Appendix I). Among those recommendations are the following:

  - **During intake, ask participants to sign "family friendly" releases** and identify family members and allies who may have positive or negative effects on their recovery.

  - **Contact approved family members and allies by phone as soon as possible,** to ask questions and solicit their involvement.

  - **Include families and allies in the service team.**

  - **Offer family and other allies ongoing support and resources or referrals.**

  - **Document all steps taken to engage families and allies.**

  - **Review this documentation** as part of quality assurance and process improvement.

  - **Give family and allies information about the agency and services, and recruit them** to serve on policy or feedback committees. *(Family inclusion and leadership)*

# Domain 2: Screening, Assessment, Service Planning and Service Delivery

## Goal G: Promote Recovery and Resilience through Evaluation and Quality Improvement

**Objective:** Solicit and use feedback from participants and families

**Potential Strategies:**

- **Conduct focus groups to solicit feedback** about participant satisfaction and improvement strategies from adults, youth and families receiving services and supports. These focus groups may be run by peers (adults, youth or families), to promote comfort and ownership and to encourage candor. *(Person- and family-directed approaches; Peer culture, support and leadership)*

- **Include an evaluation of multiple elements of recovery orientation.** Include elements such as the quality of service and support relationships, the degree of participant choice and empowerment, involvement of families and allies and the use of peer support. *(Holistic approaches toward care; Strength-based approaches that promote hope)*

- **Engage participants and families in program development and evaluation.** Continuously engage individuals (including children and youth) and families in program development and evaluation activities. *(Person- and family-directed approaches; Strength-based approaches that promote hope)*

- **Keep records of feedback.** Create a process that staff can use to record the feedback they elicit and receive from adults, youth and families concerning the quality of care they are receiving, and review this feedback with staff as part of quality assurance and quality improvement efforts. Use the evaluation data to make needed improvements to services. *(Person- and family-directed approaches)*

- **Use evaluation data to monitor health equity.** Through evaluation processes and quality improvement methods, develop policies and strategies for promoting health equity. Examine disparities in access, retention and outcomes, and address any situations in which cultural differences might be having a negative impact on experiences in care. *(Person-first [culturally competent] approaches)*

# Domain 3: Continuing Support and Early Re-intervention

## Domain Overview

Ensure a smooth transition for children, adults and families from, to, and between levels of care, other treatment services and the community.

- Ensure continuity of care through holistic continuing care planning
- Create assertive linkages and warm handoffs between levels of care and community supports
- Promote utilization of community supports
- Provide early re-intervention when needed

# Domain 3: Continuing Support and Early Re-intervention

## Background and Rationale

Continuing support and early re-intervention are critical components of behavioral health care and essential tools in sustaining wellness and enhancing long-term personal and family recovery. The term "continuing support" includes a broad range of services (e.g., face-to-face services, telephone support, mailed and e-mailed communications, mobilization of natural supports) that can be provided by professionals, peers and community-based allies.

For children and youth, this continuing support is directed as much toward the family as toward the child receiving services, because families are a critical factor in promoting children's wellness. However, for all service recipients, the emphasis is on offering continued support within the individual's and the family's natural environment, rather than solely within the treatment setting.

One role of continuing support is to identify any individuals and families who may need professional re-intervention or intensified peer support. Early re-intervention includes activities that professionals, peers and other allies may engage in to reconnect an individual to treatment and/or other support services early in the course of a recurring behavioral health challenge. For children, continuing support provides an opportunity to catch issues that arise at critical developmental points and to intervene early—within the community setting—before children's challenges reach crisis levels. This intervention may often be directed toward helping parents and other family members support the child or youth through these transitions.

Continuing care, support and early re-intervention have become standard practices in managing many chronic physical health conditions. For example, with cancer patients, recurrence is common after periods of remission. Post-treatment monitoring and support are considered essential to helping individuals with cancer sustain wellness after treatment. If there is a recurrence, post-treatment monitoring allows professionals to re-intervene early to enhance long-term recovery outcomes.

Research on recovery from alcohol dependence indicates that it takes four to five years' sustained remission before the lifetime risk of recurrence drops below 15 percent (Vaillant, 1996). The risk of resuming substance use is greatest within the first 90 days after treatment, suggesting that more assertive monitoring may be necessary—at least within this critical timeframe—to help people sustain recovery (White, 2008).

Although post-treatment monitoring and support have been shown to enhance long-term outcomes from addiction treatment significantly, only a small percentage of adolescents and adults who have completed treatment (20 to 36 percent) receive any significant amount of continuing care (White, 2008).

In contrast, the mental health community has a long history of viewing mental health challenges as chronic illnesses, but the interpretation of that belief has also posed significant challenges. The term "serious and persistent mental illness" has frequently been associated with the belief that, once one is mentally ill, there is no hope of recovery, and that mental health challenges are in fact deteriorating conditions. This belief contributed to the development of systems that inadvertently promoted dependency rather than empowering people to live full lives in their communities.

In offering care for behavioral health conditions, it is critically important that the concepts of continuing care and early re-intervention do not reinforce the notion that people with serious mental health challenges will need intensive services for the rest of their lives, or the corresponding "once a junkie, always a junkie" myth in the addiction realm (White, 2008). The truth is that people with behavioral health challenges can and do recover and achieve wellness in the context of their communities, and it is critically important to connect each individual with an array of services and supports that will help the individual and family maintain wellness and the highest quality of life possible.

Of course, the service elements needed will be different for each individual or family. For example, some continuing care plans might include a mixture of time-limited professional and non-professional forms of support, while others may choose to rely exclusively on peer- or community-based support. Not everyone with behavioral health challenges—whether these challenges include alcohol or other drug problems or mental health issues or both—will need ongoing professional support, monitoring, or intervention. Many can recover with only family and peer support.

The role of the professional is to collaborate with the individual and family to assess their recovery capital and develop a relevant and effective continuing care plan that will provide ample support and facilitate early re-intervention if the need arises. This plan should help people build their personal recovery capital, so that their wellness will be sustained more and more within their natural support systems.

In general, service reimbursement systems have not paid for post-treatment monitoring and support, so responsibility for ongoing support has been placed on individuals and families, rather than on service providers. The strategies that follow have been gathered from the literature and recommendations of providers, families and people in recovery. Going forward, DBHIDS will collaborate with providers and advocates to identify strategies to align the administrative infrastructure so that providers can more effectively and consistently provide continuing support and early re-intervention.

# Domain 3: Continuing Support and Early Re-intervention

## Goal A: Provide Integrated Services

**Objective:** Use relationships with primary care to promote ongoing wellness

**Potential Strategies:**

- **Integrate and coordinate primary care and behavioral health follow-up.** Extend collaborative relationships with primary care to provide coordinated and (wherever possible) integrated wellness check-ups. *(Holistic approaches toward care)*

- **Establish protocols for multidisciplinary monitoring of medication interactions.** Form collaborative partnerships that include behavioral health and primary care providers. Establish guidelines for communication regarding the range of medications (primary care, behavioral health) that individuals may be taking and the reality of or potential for interactions among them. *(Holistic approaches toward care)*

- **Continue to integrate with pediatric wellness checks.** Integrate behavioral health services with pediatric wellness check-ups, to continue to monitor the well being of children and youth. *(Holistic approaches toward care; Care for the needs and safety of children and adolescents)*

**Objective:** Maintain collaborative relationships with a variety of systems and providers

**Potential Strategies:**

- **Create safety within recovery support settings.** Form partnerships with a variety of recovery community organizations and assess the degree of physical and psychological safety that participants and families are likely to experience there. Assess the environments, practices and procedures of these organizations to determine their level of safety and their understanding of the needs of people with trauma histories (Harris and Fallot, 2001). *(Trauma-informed approaches)*

- **Coordinate with the range of services and supports.** Work with individuals and families to identify the services and supports that will continue to support them beyond treatment (e.g., schools, community organizations, recovery houses, faith-based organizations), to ensure that everyone is working toward the same goals of sustained wellness. Help participants negotiate differences among organizational philosophies and approaches, and assume an active advocacy stance when needed. *(Person- and family-directed approaches)*

- **Expand partnerships to respond to children's needs.** Develop the full range of partnerships with community-based services to identify and address the ongoing developmental needs of children and families. Assertively connect children and families with new sources of support. *(Care for the needs and safety of children and adolescents; Community inclusion, partnership and collaboration)*

- **Foster new peer support groups.** Encourage the development of new peer support groups within the community. Identify local institutions and organizations (e.g., places of worship, community centers, libraries, businesses) that might host community-based support groups, and link potential group facilitators with contact people within those organizations. *(Community inclusion, partnership and collaboration)*

- **Use relationships and learning exchanges with Child Protective Services** to continue cross training and coordination of assistance to participants and their families. Wherever safe and appropriate, work actively with parents in their efforts to maintain or regain custody of children who have been in protective custody. *(Care for the needs and safety of children; Trauma-informed approaches)*

# Domain 3: Continuing Support and Early Re-intervention

## Goal B: Create an Atmosphere that Promotes Strength, Recovery and Resilience

**Objective:** Celebrate resilience, recovery and wellness

Potential Strategies:

- **With input from individuals and family members, develop meaningful traditions to celebrate people's wellness**. These might include events coordinated by leadership councils, community service efforts, etc. *(Strength-based approaches that promote hope)*

- **Create opportunities for people to share their stories**. These might be facilitated within behavioral health settings, but might also include opportunities in the broader community. Activities such as these simultaneously promote hope in peers and family members and increase awareness and commitment to support resilience and recovery in other community members. *(Strength-based approaches that promote hope)*

- **Work with family members and allies to create natural environments that promote recovery and resilience**. Engage participants, families and allies in identifying the kinds of environments and the types of activities and support that promote their continued wellness. Assist people in making clear and direct requests of their natural support system, so that they play an active role in creating positive environments for themselves. *(Family inclusion and leadership)*

## Domain 3: Continuing Support and Early Re-intervention

## Goal C: Develop Inclusive, Collaborative Service Teams and Processes

**Objective:** Prepare peer support staff to facilitate mechanisms for continuing support

**Potential Strategies:**

- **Empower peer-run leadership councils to provide informal continuing support** and outreach to individuals and families who may be in need of early re-intervention. Ensure that individuals have agreed to receive support from the leadership council and that volunteers receive appropriate training in respecting individuals' and families' boundaries. *(Peer culture, support and leadership; Strength-based approaches that promote hope)*

- **Support peer-run leisure activities.** To promote continuing care and assist people in rebuilding their lives in the community, assist them in expanding their social network. These social networks can serve as an important resource to support wellness. *(Peer culture, support and leadership; Strength-based approaches that promote hope)*

- **Promote and emphasize peer-to-peer continuing support for youth.** On an ongoing basis, link adolescents with peer support groups that include other young people. Employ young adults as peer specialists to work with adolescents in developing and following continuing support plans that will help them sustain wellness after treatment. *(Care for the needs and safety of children and adolescents; Peer culture, support and leadership)*

**Objective:** Invite family members and allies to participate in the development of continuing support plans

**Potential Strategies:**

- **As appropriate, include family in the continuing care team.** Ensure that the continuing care planning and oversight process is a collaborative effort among providers, peer-based supports, the individual receiving services and (when appropriate) family members. *(Family inclusion and leadership; Person- and family-directed approaches)*

- **Support individuals in developing continuing support plans with their families.** Work collaboratively with participants to educate their family members and other important allies in ways of identifying if or when they may need to be reconnected with treatment. Work with individuals to identify the measures that would be helpful if and when early re-intervention is needed. *(Family inclusion and leadership; Person- and family-directed approaches)*

- **Work with participants to identify other members of their continuing support team *early* in the treatment process.** Rather than waiting until later stages of the treatment process, work with individuals and families early in treatment to identify the people they would like include in their continuing support team. Incorporating these individuals early in the process will provide sufficient time to deepen relationships and create a well developed network of natural support for sustained wellness. *(Family inclusion and leadership; Person- and family-directed approaches)*

**Objective:** Include primary care in team planning efforts

**Potential Strategies:**

- **As feasible and appropriate, include primary care providers in the planning process.** As directed by the individual or family, ensure that all relevant professionals, including primary care providers, are involved in a coordinated approach to ongoing support. For primary care, this might involve a plan around frequency of follow-up visits, and check-ins about behavioral health concerns during primary care visits. *(Person- and family-directed approaches; Holistic approaches toward care)*

# Domain 3: Continuing Support and Early Re-intervention

## Goal D: Provide Services, Training and Supervision that Promote Recovery and Resilience

**Objective:** Provide a menu of options to individuals and families to access continuing support

Potential Strategies:

- **Transition from professionally directed discharge plans to person- and family- directed continuing support plans.** Create an environment in which individuals and families take ownership in developing plans to sustain their wellness. Provide a diverse array of options to gain access to continuing support from professionals, peers and community based resources. (*Person- and family-directed approaches*)

- **Assist people in identifying activities that will sustain their wellness.** Encourage and support efforts to discover community-based activities that are enjoyable and that will assist in sustaining wellness. These can be integrated into continuing support plans. (*Strength-based approaches that promote hope; Holistic approaches toward care; Community inclusion, partnership and collaboration*)

- **Offer ongoing parenting education or support to both parents, as appropriate.** Invite parents to participate in parenting education and support as a support service for both mothers and fathers and/or other primary caregivers. (*Care for the needs and safety of children and adolescents; Family inclusion and leadership*)

- **Ensure that the continuing support plan is consistent with cultural identity and preferences.** Ensure that staff understand the most salient aspects of individuals' and families' cultural identities (e.g., gender, race, ethnicity, sexual orientation, spirituality), and ensure that the evolving continuing support plan is consistent with this understanding. Actively examine the ways in which the participant's and the family's cultural identities influence the continuing care options they would like, or their comfort in receiving ongoing support from existing venues. For example, in connecting an individual or family with a parent advocacy group, investigate whether or not there are other families in the organization with similar cultural backgrounds. Ask the family if this is an important consideration for its members. (*Person-first [culturally competent] approaches*)

- **Help children and youth identify and connect with support people.** Continue to assist children and youth in identifying other key sources of support (e.g., mentors, teachers, coaches, spiritual leaders, etc.) and incorporating them into their understanding of a support network. Actively work at strengthening connections with family and other key support people. *(Care for the needs and safety of children and adolescents; Holistic approaches toward care; Family inclusion and leadership)*

- **Consider cultural healers:** Explore the role of indigenous cultural healers in the individual's or the family's life, and examine the role they might play in providing continuing support. *(Person-first (culturally competent) approaches; Holistic approaches toward care)*

**Objective:** Provide training to facilitate effective continuing support and early re-intervention

**Potential Strategies:**

- **Train staff in ways of developing continuing support plans.** Prepare staff to work with participants in identifying the frequency, duration and type of continuing support that will be most effective for them. *(Strength-based approaches that promote hope)*

- **Increase staff understanding of the differences between discharge planning and continuing support plans.** *(Strength-based approaches that promote hope)*

- **Ensure that staff understand that the concept of "aftercare" is inconsistent with recovery-oriented care.** Instead create an organizational culture in which there is an ongoing commitment to providing flexible support in the quantity and duration needed. *(Strength-based approaches that promote hope)*

- **Make sure that staff are aware of the variety of continuing support options.** Give staff a list of continuing support options that are available within the organization and within the system as a whole. For example, participating in DBH/IDS's "Taking Recovery to the Streets" initiative might become a part of continuing support plan of someone who is seeking ways to participate consistently in community service. Others might choose to include visits to the Philadelphia recovery center as a part of their continuing support plans. *(Strength-based approaches that promote hope)*

- **Train staff to view the community as the primary context for healing and sustained wellness.** As a result, staff should understand that the goal of continuing care is not to continue the individual or family's connection to the treatment setting, but to deepen and expand the individual's connections in his or her natural environment that can provide sustained support in community-based settings. *(Strength-based approaches that promote hope)*

- **Train staff on ways and opportunities to utilize technology** to enhance continuing support and early re-intervention. Continuing support might start with face-to-face contact for individuals who desire higher levels of initial support and then transition to telephone-based support, texting or the internet, etc., to shift to greater levels of self-management of recovery and wellness. Technology should always be used in a manner that is consistent with professional standards of care. (*Strength-based approaches that promote hope*)

# Domain 3: Continuing Support and Early Re-intervention

## Goal E: Provide Individualized Services to Identify and Address Barriers to Wellness

**Objective:** Ensure that all organizational barriers are recognized and addressed

**Potential Strategies:**

- **Accommodate individuals' and family members' scheduling needs.** Involve all relevant parties in choosing times for continuing care and support sessions. This is particularly critical for parents of children who may be juggling limited finances, other young children, transportation issues, etc. Be flexible in your efforts to accommodate their scheduling needs. *(Family inclusion and leadership; Care for the needs and safety of children and adolescents)*

- **Overcome the barrier of limited staff availability to provide continuing support.** Maximize your engagement of volunteers to deliver ongoing monitoring and support. *(Strength-based approaches that promote hope)*

- **Attend to relationship issues that can threaten sustained wellness.** Provide couples' relapse prevention sessions during and for a period of time following treatment. *(Strength-based approaches that promote hope; Family inclusion and leadership)*

- **Help people interpret language and customs in ways that work for their recovery.** For example, some trauma survivors and some women might choose 12-Step for their addiction recovery but have difficulty reconciling the emphasis on personal "powerlessness" and "surrender" with their legitimate need for a sense of control. Staff and volunteers can lessen the confusion between these approaches by helping people distinguish between the aspects of their lives in which they have or might develop more control (e.g., their actions and reactions, their responses to stress, their choice of friends and romantic partners) and those in which they may need to accept having less control (e.g., control over whether or not they have mental health challenges, control over their reaction to alcohol or other drugs). *(Person-first [culturally competent] approaches; Peer culture, support and leadership; Trauma-informed approaches)*

# Domain 3: Continuing Support and Early Re-intervention

## Goal F: Achieve Successful Outcomes through Empirically Informed Approaches

**Objective:** Explore and use culturally appropriate, empirically informed approaches

**Potential Strategies:**

- **Promote wellness beyond active treatment.** Implement empirically supported practices such as Illness Management and Recovery to help people sustain wellness beyond a treatment episode. *(Strength-based approaches that promote hope; Holistic approaches toward care)*

- **Promote self-management.** Use emerging and promising practices such as Wellness Recovery Action Planning to promote self-management and equip people with the tools to manage their mental health and addiction challenges, both during and beyond treatment episodes. *(Strength-based approaches that promote hope; Holistic approaches toward care)*

- **Use evidence-based and promising practices to begin to rebuild meaningful lives.** As early in the care process as possible and desired by the participant, use evidence-based practices such as Support Employment and Supported Education to assist people in creating the quality of life that they desire. *(Strength-based approaches that promote hope)*

- **Continue to use empirically informed practices to further the recovery orientation.** Make use of the growing body of empirically supported approaches. Continue to use solution-focused approaches such as motivational interviewing and incentive-based models such as contingency management to increase people's motivation for recovery. *(Strength-based approaches that promote hope)*

# Domain 3: Continuing Support and Early Re-intervention

## Goal G: Promote Recovery and Resilience through Evaluation and Quality Improvement

**Objective:** Solicit and use feedback from participants, alumni and families

**Potential Strategies:**

- **Conduct focus groups to solicit feedback** about participant and alumni satisfaction with continuing care and support services, and to brainstorm improvement strategies. These focus groups may be run by peers (adults, youth, or families) to promote comfort and ownership and to encourage candor. *(Person- and family-directed approaches; Peer culture, support and leadership)*

- **Engage participants, alumni and families in evaluation of continuing care.** Continuously engage individuals (including children and youth) and families in the development and evaluation of ongoing services. Include outcome data on the success of follow-up and early re-engagement efforts. *(Person- and family-directed approaches; Peer culture, support and leadership)*

- **Develop evaluation procedures that track the provision of empirically supported approaches to continuing support.** For example, for addiction treatment services, track the percentage of individuals who receive 5 or more contacts in the first 90 days following discharge, since this is associated with improved outcomes.

- **Use evaluation processes to identify individuals' and families' preferences regarding types of continuing support.** For example do most clients prefer in-person continuing support, peer-based support in the community, technology based continuing support strategies? This data can be used to continue to enhance services in the future.

- **Use quantitative and qualitative evaluation approaches to identify barriers** to participation in available continuing support services, and to measure participants' satisfaction with continuing support services.

# Domain 4: Community Connection and Mobilization

## Domain Overview

To have communities that understand, assist and support children, adults and families with behavioral health needs.

- Create and educate communities to promote recovery, resilience and the development of protective factors
- Increase the use of natural supports to assist individuals in prevention, early intervention, reconnection to treatment and providing alternative pathways to recovery and resilience
- Create seamless relationships between the treatment system and the broader community by way of bi-directional referrals and collaborations

# Section III: Strategies in the Four Domains

# Domain 4: Community Connection and Mobilization

## Background and Rationale

A recovery- and resilience-oriented system is committed to supporting people in their efforts to move beyond their problems and challenges to the development of full and meaningful lives in the community. Not only is this web of supportive and fulfilling connections essential to their long-term recovery, but it is also their right by law.

The right to meaningful inclusion in the community is embedded in the 1990 Americans with Disabilities Act (ADA) and affirmed by the Supreme Court's 1999 *Olmstead* decision. The unnecessary institutionalization of individuals who could live in the community with the proper supports is a violation of their rights. The 2003 final report of the President's New Freedom Commission on Mental Health further reinforced the notion of community inclusion and recovery as major policy goals for the design and delivery of behavioral health care (DBH/MRS, 2006).

The need to open the door to full and meaningful community involvement is a central challenge for behavioral health systems, whose traditional focus has been on the provision of site-based services. Connecting people with full involvement requires that providers discover the hopes and dreams of individuals who have experienced mental health and/or substance-related challenges, and use the assets of these individuals, their families and their communities to enable them to fulfill their hopes and dreams.

A transformed system also addresses the fact that the health of individuals is affected by the health of the overall community. Provider agencies exist within the community. They are members of the community and therefore have a responsibility to participate in—and assist in improving—the overall health of the community.

Throughout most of the field's history, the behavioral health system viewed community involvement and connection as something that happened at, or close to, the end of treatment—depending on adherence and symptom remission and control.

- Systems did not view the community as capable of promoting people's health, but as a place where people might be released when they were "healthier."
- People were told to wait until they had achieved abstinence or

stability before they pursued educational opportunities, volunteer activities, employment, etc.

- Children were viewed in isolation from their family, peer and social contexts.
- Treatment professionals did not consider the totality of the individual's environment in formulating diagnoses and treatment decisions.
- The individual's immediate community (e.g., family, key allies, spiritual resources) was seldom invited into assessment, planning or service-delivery processes.
- Community connections or "linkages" were considered the purview of the case manager—and even then were done as referrals rather than as "warm handoffs" or intentional connections to these resources.
- Providers developed resources within their agencies, even if those resources already existed in the naturally occurring community.
- Agencies were often seen as places of retreat from the unsafe community, rather than as places to learn skills to navigate more successfully in the world.

In the field's early days, many community-based providers were just that, **community** providers. There was a community services funding stream that supported many of the services that are envisioned for Philadelphia's transformed system. Over time, due to changes in funding, many have lost this original connection to their communities and have become institution based, with few connections with the surrounding community. For the transformation of these systems, it is critical that these connections be strengthened, and DBHIDS is committed to examining ways of aligning the policy and fiscal infrastructure to support providers in promoting community connections and mobilizing community support.

Transformed systems both acknowledge and make full use of the community's role as the individual's and the family's home, and potential as a place of both challenge and healing. In transformed agencies, leadership recognizes the critical need for vibrant, reciprocal community partnerships in supporting the recovery and resilience of the individual—and of the entire community.

The kinds of connections that must be forged will vary across levels of care. For example, inpatient units will connect with the community primarily through active engagement of family members, allies and community-based providers. Community-based providers can and must have strong connections with the communities in which they are located. In a system that includes mutually beneficial connections between communities and agencies, the work of direct service providers becomes easier. Because the actions and attitudes of agencies and their staff are so crucial to the development of community connections, the strategies presented here include both those that apply to executive leadership and those that apply to individual providers.

As one provider noted: "*Many people I deal with have been living in Philadelphia their whole life and do not know anything about what is available to them in the community.*" Other participants in the development of these guidelines reinforced the importance of this simple but central point: "*If you don't know what's in the community, you can't do much; you need to know where things are and how you can get to them.*"

A seamless connection between the professional services that an individual receives and the community in which he or she lives is a prerequisite for sustained positive outcomes in real-life situations. Community connection must be a feature of all facets of service planning and delivery. As in the other domains, integrating some of the strategies identified will require collaboration between DBHIDS and the provider and advocacy communities, to align key administrative functions and fiscal strategies

# Domain 4: Community Connection and Mobilization

## Goal A: Provide Integrated Services

**Objective:** Strengthen partnerships with primary care providers to promote community connection

**Potential Strategies:**

- **Identify key primary care partners.** Develop relationships with neighborhood-based FQHCs and other local health care practices, and ensure that each person receiving services is connected to a primary care partner during the course of treatment. (*Community inclusion, partnership and collaboration; Holistic approaches toward care*)

  - **Identify obstacles to collaboration** with primary care providers.

  - **Address obstacles** that can be solved through changes to organizational policies, procedures and staff training and communicate more systemic obstacles to DBHIDS for additional attention.

  - **Explore the ways in which various staff roles might be modified or expanded** to facilitate more participant connections with primary care settings.

    - **Use transparent, participatory processes to explore with staff how the roles of peers might be expanded** to include assertive outreach to primary care settings, and to provide peer support within the context of primary care settings.

    - **Examine how the roles of clinicians might be expanded** to provide brief intervention services within primary care settings.

  - **Assertively seek to identify the most pressing concerns of local primary care providers** regarding behavioral health services. These concerns might include:

    - Lack of timely access to services due to long waiting lists.

    - Limited follow-up after referrals are made.

  - **Create opportunities for dialogue with staff and primary care providers** to explore possibilities of bi-directional service integration that would address identified concerns and increase people's connections to this important community resource.

  - **Provide training to Primary Care professionals about working with peer and non-professional community providers.**

**Objective:** Identify ways to strengthen and mobilize additional community-based recovery supports for people with behavioral health challenges

**Potential Strategies:**

- **Identify tools that can support community-building efforts.** Asset Based Community Development (ABCD) is a model that can be used to assist with conducting community asset mapping (Kretzmann & McKnight, 1993). This is the process of intentionally identifying the human, material, financial, entrepreneurial and other resources in the local community that can support your efforts.

  - **Identify the gifts, skills and capacities of people living in your community** that can be mobilized to support community integration

  - **Identify and reach out to the citizens' associations** within your community to increase both awareness and support of people with behavioral health challenges; and

  - **Identify the local organizations and institutions** you might partner with to support community integration efforts. These include small and large businesses in your neighborhood, hospitals, educational institutions, human service organizations, etc.

  Examine the extent to which you can develop mutually beneficial partnerships with these local entities. For example, partner with a local small business to develop apprenticeship opportunities. *(Community inclusion, partnership and collaboration)*

- **Foster new peer support groups in the community.** Encourage the development of new peer support groups within the community. Identify local institutions and organizations (e.g., places of worship, community centers, libraries, businesses) that might host community-based support groups, and link potential group facilitators with contact people within those organizations. *(Peer culture, support and leadership; Community inclusion, partnership and collaboration)*

- **Update community resource files**; focus on community resources in staff/team meetings; and encourage staff to bring information about any newly discovered resources to a central location where this information can be maintained, updated and shared among staff and participants. *(Person-first [culturally competent] approaches; Community inclusion, partnership and collaboration*

# Domain 4: Community Connection and Mobilization

## Goal B: Create an Atmosphere that Promotes Strength, Recovery and Resilience

**Objective:** Foster a sense of hope and resilience throughout the community

Potential Strategies:

- **Join and initiate efforts to decrease stigma throughout all service systems.** Convey to all partners in the community, and to the community as a whole, a strong and consistent message that behavioral health challenges are illnesses; that recovery is possible; that people with these challenges have strength, worth and dignity; that discrimination is unacceptable; and that people with these conditions have a right to meaningful and fulfilling lives in the community. *(Strength-based approaches that promote hope; Community inclusion, partnership and collaboration; Peer culture, support and leadership)*
  - Use community media and public information outlets to provide accurate public education.
  - Participate in local neighborhood meetings
  - Provide technical assistance to organizations that want to be involved in public education efforts.

**Objective:** Increase the visibility and advocacy capacity of people in recovery in your local community

Potential Strategies:

- **Refer interested individuals and family members to the free family and peer storytelling trainings.** These trainings, hosted by DBHIDS will increase people's comfort and confidence in sharing their stories in public settings. They also provide a networking opportunity and assist people in building a natural network of peer support outside of their treatment setting. *(Strength-based approaches that promote hope; Community inclusion, partnership and collaboration)*
- **Identify additional mechanisms to support the presentation skills of those who are interested in sharing their stories.** These might include the First Fridays series hosted by DBHIDS, opportunities to present to staff and peers within your agency, opportunities to present to local primary care partners about the kinds of services and supports that would be helpful, etc. *(Strength-based approaches that promote hope; Community inclusion, partnership*

*and collaboration)*

- Collaborate with organizations identified through your community asset mapping efforts to host public awareness events. *(Strength-based approaches that promote hope; Community inclusion, partnership and collaboration)*

**Transformation Practice Guidelines**
Philadelphia DBHIDS

# Domain 4: Community Connection and Mobilization

## Goal C: Develop Inclusive, Collaborative Service Teams and Processes

**Objective:** Use the skills and experience of staff and volunteers strategically

Potential Strategies:

- **Use the knowledge of stakeholders to develop a community resource file.** Use the experiences of staff, participants, peers, families and allies in the community to continually update and expand knowledge of potential resources and partners in the community. *(Strength-based approaches that promote hope; Community inclusion, partnership and collaboration)*

- **Use staff and volunteers to build a bridge from clinical care to the community:** Use staff and volunteers strategically to provide a living bridge between the learning that takes place within the clinical setting and that which takes place in the natural community. *(Strength-based approaches that promote hope; Peer culture, support and leadership; Community inclusion, partnership and collaboration).* Whenever possible:

  - **Have staff accompany participants into the community,** to promote the transfer of new skills into the natural environment.

  - **Have staff and participants collaborate in developing plans** for their experiences in the community, with staff follow-up to learn how the experience went and support the development of next steps.

  - **Involve peers in this process, and use peer support as another bridge** to the natural community. Use peer specialists and peer recovery coaches to provide assertive links with supports in the community, to the extent that individuals and families choose these opportunities. Peers can help individuals and families identify their existing long-term support systems in the community, evaluate the health and effectiveness of these systems and develop new supports as necessary. *(Peer culture, support and leadership; Community inclusion, partnership and collaboration)*

- **Continue to develop peers' ability to lead support groups.** Encourage interested peers to participate in training on self-help group facilitation. *(Peer culture, support and leadership; Strength-based approaches that promote hope)*

**Objective:** Use the service team to promote positive community connections for children

Potential Strategies:

- **Use the team to help children and youth identify and connect with key sources of support in the community** (e.g., mentors, teachers, coaches, spiritual leaders) and incorporate these resources into their understanding of a support network. Throughout the service period, actively work at strengthening connections with family and other key support people, and with the community as a whole. (*Community inclusion, partnership and collaboration; Care for the needs and safety of children and adolescents*)

# Domain 4: Community Connection and Mobilization

## Goal D: Provide Services, Training and Supervision that Promote Recovery and Resilience

**Objective:** Take a person, family and community-centered approach

**Potential Strategies:**

- **Understand people—particularly children and youth—in context.** Train and support all staff in viewing individuals, and their behaviors and choices, in the context of their broader family and community. For example, what appears to be symptomatic in a child or youth (e.g., denial, lack of trust, acting out in school or at home) may be adaptive to the environment and represent the child's or youth's best way of coping with and managing a difficult situation. *(Care for the needs and safety of children and adolescents; Person-first [culturally competent] approaches; Community inclusion, partnership and collaboration)*

- **Focus on children's developing adaptation to their environments.** As children and youth continue to grow and develop, ensure that staff continue to identify, engage and align with new, age-appropriate resources within their natural environments; to identify points of challenge; and to mobilize support and re-engage them in services if and when it becomes necessary. *(Strength-based approaches that promote hope; Care for the needs and safety of children and adolescents; Community inclusion, partnership and collaboration; Trauma-informed approaches)*

- **Trace the history of community connections, including cultural connections.** Explore with people the nature of their past connections with the community, their families' patterns of connecting with the community and their desire for the kinds of connections that would be meaningful to them. *(Strength-based approaches that promote hope; Community inclusion, partnership and collaboration; Person-first [culturally competent] approaches)*

**Objective:** Provide staff/volunteer education on community resources

**Potential Strategies:**

- **Expand staff vision beyond clinical resources.** Help providers conceptualize their knowledge base broadly, to include the critical knowledge of local resources and ways of connecting people with those resources. *(Person-first [culturally competent] approaches; Community inclusion, partnership and collaboration)*

- **Have staff work with participants to develop their personal community resource maps,** based on the organization's assessment and identification of local resources. Through this collaborative process, staff and participants identify all relevant community-based resources to support participants' and families' goals in a variety of life domains long after treatment is complete. Resources might include youth recreation centers and mentoring programs, support networks at school, parent advocacy groups, communities of recovery, professional advocacy groups, libraries, recovery support centers, indigenous healers and institutions (e.g., folk healers, faith-based supports), supportive friends and family members, etc. For children and youth, forge connections with school systems, and have resources in place for advocacy support, in case any issues arise. *(Holistic approaches toward care; Community inclusion, partnership and collaboration)*

- **Track participants' efforts at community integration.** Have staff and participants collaborate in monitoring and refining plans for ongoing support and involvement in the community, with staff follow-up to learn how these experiences went and support the development of next steps. Wherever possible, involve peers in this process, so that support is available in the natural community. *(Person-first [culturally competent] approaches; Person- and family-directed approaches)*

- **Know both positive and negative influences:** Ensure that staff are aware of all resources and influences in participants' lives, both positive and negative. Ask people to teach you about their worlds. *(Strength-based approaches that promote hope; Community inclusion, partnership and collaboration)*

- **Explore cultural resources in the community.** Gather and provide information about culturally meaningful groups and organizations in the community that individuals might join and share in a collective identity. Possibilities include fraternities/ sororities, fraternal organizations, block or neighborhood organizations and organizations based specific cultural characteristics (e.g., ethnicity, gender, sexual orientation, age). *(Person-first [culturally competent] approaches; Community inclusion, partnership and collaboration)*

- **Educate staff and volunteers on community resources.** Ensure that staff and volunteers stay current on all of the identified community resources and provide opportunities that will help them continue to learn more about these and other available resources. Continue to update community resource files; focus on community resources in staff/team meetings; and encourage staff to bring information about any newly discovered resources to a central location where this information can be maintained, updated and shared among staff and participants. *(Person-first [culturally* *competent] approaches; Community inclusion, partnership and collaboration)*

**Objective:** Take a multi-faceted approach toward connection for support

**Potential Strategies:**

- **Ensure that such connections are made well before treatment ends.** Assertively connect adults, youth and families to a broad range of community-based supports (driven by their needs and preferences) during treatment, rather than passively referring them toward the end of the treatment episode. *(Recovery-oriented clinical and organizational services; Community inclusion, partnership and collaboration)*

- **Include groups and peer support in service plans.** In service plans, include group modalities that take place in natural settings such as communities, schools, etc. (e.g., life-skills groups, psychoeducational groups, family support groups, teen peer groups), and take advantage of the natural peer support that develops. *(Holistic approaches toward care; Peer culture, support and leadership; Community inclusion, partnership and collaboration)*

**Objective:** Connect people with opportunities to expand their lives and abilities

**Potential Strategies:**

- **Help people find education and employment opportunities.** Train staff to understand the impact of the poverty of opportunity that many people experience, limiting their ideas, energy and ability to identify their interests. *(Strength-based approaches that promote hope; Community inclusion, partnership. and collaboration).* For example:

  *Providers need to know what is going on in the community, particularly for youth. The problem is, if no one at home cares about me, then the community is the next place to go, and that may lead to bad things. You go where you get respect and feel powerful, which may be a gang in the community. Therapists need to understand that the community does affect us.*
  *—Youth*

  - **Provide for community exposure opportunities,** recognizing that exposure to new possibilities is often the first step toward identifying interests and strengths.

  - **Focus on creating or expanding access to opportunities** for people to pursue their aspirations as individuals, as breadwinners and as community members.

- **Promote community service and involvement.** Recognize, support and encourage the process of "giving back" to the community as a key mechanism for healing, recovery, self-worth and community connection. *(Strength-based approaches that promote hope; Peer culture, support and leadership; Community inclusion, partnership and collaboration)*. For example:

- **Encourage natural ways of being good neighbors** (e.g., cleaning up the street in the neighborhood, planting flowers, participating in local development committee opportunities).

- **Develop formalized volunteer roles with others in the community.**

- **Match participants with community and civic organizations** in their communities.

- **Support participation in "citizenship" activities**, including voting, advocacy of meaningful causes, staging public celebrations, attending meetings of neighborhood associations/ block clubs/watches and helping with block clean-up efforts.

- **Promote safe, sober and fulfilling activities in the community.** For people with substance use disorders, help them learn and gain access to new ways of having fun and enjoying life without using alcohol or other drugs, and provide opportunities to exercise these new skills. Include in this exploration their choice of faith-based/ spiritual resources (both organized institutions and spiritual/ indigenous healers). *(Strength-based approaches that promote hope; Holistic approaches toward care; Community inclusion, partnership and collaboration)*

- **Continue to promote a holistic approach to community involvement.** Support connections with activities that match the full range of people's interests. Examples offered by focus group participants included: *"get[ting] involved in other things like knitting, artwork, etc."*; the *"women [who] started a movement with the jogging program"*; and *"learn[ing] more about the community by cutting grass, cleaning the street, get[ting] into motion."* These can include other alternative approaches (e.g., yoga and tai chi classes, community gardening organizations). *(Holistic approaches toward care; Community inclusion, partnership and collaboration)*

*"Expertise in one aspect does not guarantee expertise in other areas—either for the practitioner or the person in recovery: Many folks who are in programs have degrees but do not have the mechanisms to help them find employment."*
—Person in Recovery

# Domain 4: Community Connection and Mobilization

## Goal E: Provide Individualized Services to Identify and Address Barriers to Wellness

**Objective:** Ensure that all organizational barriers are recognized and addressed

Potential Strategies:

- **Facilitate community inclusion, partnership and collaboration as soon as possible.** Eliminate exclusionary criteria that require adults and "transition age" youth to achieve stability or maintain abstinence before they can pursue a life in the community. Instead, work as quickly as possible to facilitate supportive and meaningful community inclusion, partnership and collaboration. *(Strength-based approaches that promote hope; Community inclusion, partnership and collaboration)*

- **Identify barriers to promoting community inclusion.** As you work to promote community inclusion, track systemic barriers encountered and communicate these to DBHIDS for collaborative system alignment.

**Objective:** Address safety issues in ongoing support services

Potential Strategies:

- **Continue to monitor safety in the family and the community.** Continue to monitor and address the sense of safety or danger that people experience in their families and communities. Use assessments to identify any pre-immigration trauma in participants' countries of origin that might affect their ability to connect with their current community. *(Trauma-informed approaches; Person-first [culturally competent] approaches; Community inclusion, partnership and collaboration)*

- **Build safety in the family and the community:** Provide ongoing family support and develop safe options for making community connections (e.g., going to community activities with a group of safe and supportive peers, choosing recovery meetings whose members are of a particular gender or ethnicity). This process begins with a collaborative exploration (in concrete terms) of the range of alternatives participants might have for making safe connections. *(Trauma-informed approaches; Person-first [culturally competent] approaches; Family inclusion and leadership; Community inclusion, partnership and collaboration)*

# Domain 4: Community Connection and Mobilization

## Goal F: Achieve Successful Outcomes through Empirically Informed Approaches

**Objective:** Explore and use culturally appropriate, empirically informed approaches

Potential Strategies:

- **Use evidence-based practices to help people find employment.** Use practices such as *supported education* and *supported employment* to help people find competitive employment. *(Strength-based approaches that promote hope; Community inclusion, partnership and collaboration)*

- **Where limited evidence exists to determine empirically informed approaches, ask individuals and families** what strategies might help support their increased engagement in the community. *(Person and family-driven approaches)*

- **Familiarize staff with Asset Based Community Development Approaches.** These strategies promote the development of healthy communities by finding and mobilizing the local strengths rather than focusing on the deficits. *(Strength-based approaches that promote hope; Community inclusion, partnership and collaboration)*

# Domain 4: Community Connection and Mobilization

## Goal G: Promote Recovery and Resilience through Evaluation and Quality Improvement

**Objective:** Evaluate the effectiveness of community services and connections

Potential Strategies:

- **Use focus groups and other evaluation measures to solicit feedback** about participant and alumni satisfaction with the community connection process and community services, and with the forms of support used during continuing care, and to brainstorm improvement strategies. Include evaluation of the safety and appropriateness of the community resources used. Focus groups may be run by peers (adults, youth, or families), to promote comfort and ownership and to encourage candor. *(Person-first [culturally competent] approaches; Strength-based approaches that promote hope; Person- and family-directed approaches; Community inclusion, partnership and collaboration)*

**Objective:** Evaluate outreach to and involvement of the community

Potential Strategies:

- **Design community-friendly ways of evaluating community collaboration.** Evaluate community partners' comfort with and enthusiasm for their relationships and collaborative efforts with treatment and recovery support organizations. *(Person-first [culturally competent] approaches; Community inclusion, partnership and collaboration)*
- **Track the number of service units delivered offsite in non-treatment settings:**
    - **Track the percentage of participants whose family or other allies become involved** (among those who want family members involved in their services).
    - **Evaluate the extent to which participants are satisfied with their sense of belonging in their community**
    - **Track the extent to which participants feel that they have productive roles or are involved in meaningful activities in their communities** (e.g. volunteering, employment, educational opportunities, recreational pursuits, etc.)

# Appendices

**A:** References

**B:** Toward a Clear Understanding of Recovery and Resilience

**C:** Implementing Evidence-based Practices

**D:** Trauma-informed Care: From Survival to Thriving

**E:** Diversity of Strengths

**F:** Areas of Inquiry When Conducting a Person-first Assessment

**G:** DBHIDS Policy on Services to LGBTQI People

**H:** Blue Ribbon Commission Goals and Recommendations

**I:** Family Resource Network Family Involvement Best Practice Guidelines

**J:** Person-first Best Practice Guidelines

# Appendix A

# References

AACAP, 2007. *Practice parameters for the psychiatric assessment of children and adolescents (AACAP, 46:2 Supplement, February 2007)*. Washington, DC: American Academy of Child and Adolescent Psychiatry.

Achara-Abrahams,I., Evans, A., King, J.K. (2010). Recovery focused behavioral health care system transformation: A framework for change and lessons learned. In Kelly, J. & White, W. *Addiction recovery management: Theory, science and practice*. New York: Springer Science.

Davidson, L., Drake, R., Schmutte, T., Dinzeo, T., and Andres-Hyman, R. (2009). Oil and water or oil and vinegar? Evidence-based medicine meets recovery. *Community Mental Health Journal, 45*:323-332.

DBH/MRS (2006). Community Integration, *Tools for Transformation* Series. Philadelphia, PA: Department of Behavioral Health and Mental Retardation Services.

DHHS (2003). *New Freedom Commission on Mental Health: Achieving the promise: transforming mental health care in America. Final Report*. DHHS Pub. No. SMA-03–3832. Rockville MD, Department of Health and Human Services, 2003. (Available at www.mentalhealthcommission.gov/reports/finalreport/fullreport-02.htm)

Family Resource Network (2010). *Standards for a model approach to involving consumer-identified "significant people" in mental health treatment and recovery programs*. Philadelphia, PA: Philadelphia Family Resource Network, Mental Health Association and Philadelphia Department of Behavioral Health and Intellectual disAbility Services.

Harris, M., & Fallot, R.D. (Eds.) (2001). *Using trauma theory to design service systems: New directions for mental health services*. New York: Jossey-Bass.

Harrison, M.E., McKay, M.M., & Bannon, W.M. (2004). Inner-city child mental health service use: The real question is why youth and families do not use services. *Community Mental Health Journal*, 40(2), 119-131

Hser, Y., Anglin, M., Grella, C., Longshore, D., & Prendergast, M. (1997). Drug treatment careers: A conceptual framework and existing research findings. *Journal of Substance Abuse Treatment, 14*(3),543-558.

Institute of Medicine (2001). *Crossing the quality chasm: A new health system for the 21st century*. Washington, DC: National Academies Press.

Institute of Medicine (2006). *Improving the quality of health care for mental and substance-use conditions*. Washington, DC: National Academies Press.

Institute of Medicine (2009). *Preventing mental, emotional, and behavioral disorders among young people: Progress and possibilities*. Washington, DC: National Academies Press.

Kretzmann, J.P., & McKnight, J.L. (1993). *Building communities from the inside out: A path toward finding and mobilizing a community's assets*. Evanston, IL: Institute for Policy Research.

Mayor's Blue Ribbon Commission (2007). *The Mayor's Blue Ribbon Commission on Children's Behavioral Health, Final Report*. Philadelphia, PA: Blue Ribbon Commission on Children's Behavioral Health

McKay, M.M., Stoewe, J., McCadam, K. & Gonzales, J. (1998). Increasing access to child mental health services for urban children and their care givers. *Health and Social Work, 23,* 9-15.

Melle, I., Larsen, T.K., Haahr, U., Friis, S., Johannessen, J.O., Opjordsmoen, S., Simonsen, E., Rund, B.R., Vaglum, P., McGlashan, T. (2004). Reducing the duration of untreated first episode psychosis: Effects on clinical presentation. *Archives of General Psychiatry,*61, 143-150.

Moos, R.H., & Moos, B.S. (2003). Long-term influence of duration and intensity of treatment on previously untreated individuals with alcohol use disorders. *Addiction, 98,* 325-337.

Moos, R. H., & Moos, B. S. (2003). Risk factors for nonremission among initially untreated individuals with alcohol use disorders. *Journal of Studies on Alcohol, 64,* 555-563.

OMHSAS (2005). *A call for change: Toward a recovery-oriented mental health service system for adults.* Pennsylvania Department of Public Welfare, Office of Mental Health and Substance Abuse Services.

Substance Abuse and Mental Health Services Administration. (2003). *Results from the 2002 National Survey on Drug Use and Health: National findings* (Office of Applied Studies, NHSDA Series H-22, DHHS Publication No. SMA 03–3836). Rockville, MD.

Substance Abuse and Mental Health Services Administration. (2006). *National Survey on Drug Use and Health.* Washington, DC. Accessed on May 8, 2011 at: http://www.commonwealthfund.org/Content/Performance-Snapshots/Unmet-Needs-for-Health-Care/Unmet-Need-for-Mental-Health-Care--Adults.aspx

Substance Abuse and Mental Health Services Administration. (2007). *Results from the 2006 National Survey on Drug Use and Health: National findings* (Office of Applied Studies, NSDUH Series H-32, DHHS Publication No. SMA 07-4293). Rockville, MD.

Szapocznik, J., Perez-Vidal, A., Brickman, A., Foote, F. H., Santisteban, D., Hervis, O., & Kurtines, W. H. (1988). Engaging adolescent drug abusers and their families into treatment: A strategic structural systems approach. *Journal of Consulting and Clinical Psychology: 552-557.*

Vaillant, G.E. (1996). A long-term follow-up of male alcohol abuse. *Archives of General Psychiatry, 53:*243-249.

Wallace, A.E. & Weeks, W.B. (2004). Substance abuse intensive outpatient treatment: Does program graduation matter? *Journal of Substance Abuse Treatment, 27,* 27-30.

White, W., and Cloud, W. (2008). Recovery capital: A primer for addiction professionals. *Counselor, 9*(5):22-27.

White, W.L. (2008). *Recovery management and recovery-oriented systems of care: Scientific rationale and promising practices.* Pittsburgh, PA: Northeast Addiction Technology Transfer Center, Great Lakes Addiction Technology Transfer Center, Philadelphia Department of Behavioral Health & Mental Retardation Services.

# Appendix B

# Toward a Clear Understanding of Recovery and Resilience

Words like "recovery" and "resilience" are easy to bend, stretch and apply to almost any type of practice. To avoid any such distortion, the guideline-development process has built on the earlier work of the Philadelphia Recovery Advisory Committee and the Mayor's Blue Ribbon Commission on Children's Behavioral Health. The guidelines are rooted in the definitions of recovery and resilience developed by stakeholders in these two bodies. The recovery definition was crafted by the Recovery Advisory Committee:

---

### Recovery Definition

**Recovery Advisory Committee, City of Philadelphia DBHIDS**

*Recovery is the process of pursuing a fulfilling and contributing life regardless of the difficulties one has faced. It involves not only the restoration but continued enhancement of a positive identity and personally meaningful connections and roles in one's community. Recovery is facilitated by relationships and environments that provide hope, empowerment, choices and opportunities that promote people reaching their full potential as individuals and community members.*

---

A number of processes contributed to the city's shared understanding of resilience. DBH/MRS conducted a series of focus groups with providers, advocates, family members and youth, to explore key factors in the promotion of resilience in children and adolescents, and held a resilience conference in which local youth, families and national experts shared their perspectives. In addition, the work of the Mayor's Blue Ribbon Commission has had a major influence on the development of this understanding of resilience (see Appendix H, "Blue Ribbon Commission Values").

---

### Resilience Definition

*Resilience is a protective process which enables us to cope effectively when we are faced with significant adversities. It is a dynamic process that can change across time, developmental stage and life domain. All children, youth, adults, families and communities have the capacity to demonstrate resilience. There are many factors that enhance a child's resilience pathway, including:*

- *positive relationships with caregivers, peers or a caring adult*

- *internal strengths such as problem-solving skills, determination and hope*

- *environmental factors like effective schools and communities*

---

DBHMRS synthesized the definition of resilience shown on the previous page from the Blue Ribbon Commission's findings, with additional input from local stakeholders and national experts.

Both the recovery and resilience definitions reflect the stakeholders' personal and professional understanding that each of these concepts is centered on the ability to return to optimal levels of functioning in spite of challenging or threatening circumstances. With these definitions at the foundation, the collaborative development of these practice guidelines found a stronger and steadier course.

Its experience with recovery and resilience is one of the best elements that the behavioral health community has to offer our nation's health care reform efforts. Forging, embracing and providing a real-life forum for clearer and stronger definitions of recovery and resilience will have benefits throughout Philadelphia's transformation efforts, and far beyond.

# Appendix C

# Implementing Evidence-based Practices

## DEPARTMENT OF BEHAVIORAL HEALTH AND INTELLECTUAL DISABILITY SERVICES

## CITY OF PHILADELPHIA

### The Rationale for Utilizing Evidence-Based Practices

The Surgeon General's Report on Mental Health (1999) indicated that "critical gaps exist between those who need service and those who receive services…between optimally effective treatment and what many individuals receive in actual practice settings." This report, along with a document released by the Institute of Medicine (2001), highlighted the finding that despite extensive evidence that demonstrates the effectiveness of particular behavioral health practices, these practices are not routinely integrated into behavioral health settings. In fact, research indicates that it takes approximately 15 years for scientific practice to become incorporated into health care settings.

A core value of The Department of Behavioral Health and Intellectual disAbility Services is that a recovery-oriented and resilience-oriented system of care is one that provides the highest quality and most effective behavioral health services to consumers and persons in recovery. As such, we are committed to developing a system of care that is grounded in evidence-based practices. The Department recognizes that this shift will be a developmental process. Research shows that training and education alone do not have a significant influence on practice behaviors. Consequently, to continue our pursuit of this goal, DBH/IDS will align resources, policies, and technical assistance to support the ongoing transformation of our system to one that promotes and routinely utilizes evidence-based practices. This document will provide a brief description of DBH/IDS's approach to evidence based practices and provide recommendations for incorporating them into practice settings.

### What are Evidence-Based Practices?

The term evidence-based practice has been referred to as the process of "turning knowledge into practice." The idea is to convert what we know based on scientific evidence into what we do. One of the most popular definitions is: "Evidence based practices are interventions for which there is consistent scientific evidence showing that they improve client outcomes." The Department, however, recognizes that there are numerous challenges to implementing EBPs in the real world. Among these are: implementing new strategies with limited resources, attempting to utilize practices that are not normed on populations similar to the population being served in Philadelphia, and the fact that many community-based organizations that achieve excellent outcomes do not have the resources to conduct empirically based studies that validate the evidence base of their services.

As a result of these real world challenges, the DBHIDS endorses an expanded view of evidence which not only acknowledges that evidence occurs on a continuum, but also emphasizes the importance of the role that consumers and family members play in identifying which services are most effective for them. Consequently, **the definition of EBPs subscribed to by the Department is "practical and specific clinical interventions and supports that are designed for specific groups of people in a particular setting and that are determined in collaboration with consumers to enhance their recovery."**

As the scientific evidence that supports clinical practices is often inadequate or incomplete, DBH is using the following four categories to assess the levels/types of evidence that support proposed practices.

**Levels of Evidence**

# Evidence Based

- Interventions which have a <u>body</u> of controlled studies and where at least one meta-analysis shows strong support for the practice.
- Results have a high level of confidence, due to the randomized control methodology

  **Example:** A series of randomized controlled trials comparing supported employment (also referred to as "IPS, Individual Placement and Support") with a variety of traditional, "step-wise" vocational programs has clearly established supported employment as a highly effective intervention. This intervention results in significant gains in competitive employment rates, earned income levels, and employment tenure among individuals with severe behavioral health disorders.

# Evidence Supported

- Interventions that have demonstrated effectiveness through quasi-experimental studies (e.g., "Time Series" studies or detailed program evaluations that include data on the impact of the programs or interventions).
- Data from administrative databases or quality improvement programs that shed light on the impact of the program or intervention.
- Interventions that may have a single controlled study that shows effectiveness, but the results haven't been replicated or demonstrated with the populations of interest.
- Program evaluations that provide strong evidence of the effectiveness of an intervention or clinical approach (e.g., cohort management strategies)

  **Example:** As one component of a quality improvement program in a local mental health authority, an in-service training program for providers and consumers/people in recovery was offered regarding the use of strategies to improve the collaborative, person-centered nature of treatment planning. Pre-post data collected prior to and after the training intervention indicated significant improvements in consumer satisfaction and consumers' level of participation in treatment planning.

## Evidence Informed

- Evidence of the effectiveness of an intervention is inferred based on a limited amount of supporting data.
- Based on data derived from the replication of an EBP that has been modified or adapted to meet the needs of a specific population.
- This data is fed back into the system. New interventions are developed, traditional interventions are modified, and ineffective interventions are eliminated.
- Provides a template/framework for other systems to modify their programs and interventions.

  **Example:** MET has been shown to be a highly effective approach for engaging people into treatment. While no studies have examined the use of MET specifically with African American men, based on the overall effectiveness of MET, it is reasonable to extrapolate and pilot this approach within this population. Data from the pilot will determine if extrapolation was an appropriate decision and identify potential MET modifications necessary for the specific population of African American men.

## Evidence Suggested

- Consensus driven, or based on agreement among experts.
- Based on values or a philosophical framework derived from experience, but may not yet have a strong basis of support in research meeting standards for scientific rigor.
- Provides a context for understanding the process by which outcomes occur.
- Based on qualitative data, e.g., ethnographic observations.

  **Example:** Experience has shown us the importance of Culturally Competent and Recovery-Oriented Care, yet scientific evidence lags behind the expert and values-based and anecdotal consensus regarding the effectiveness of these approaches.

This expanded view of evidence based practices encourages providers to not only become aware of the level of evidence that supports the utilization of a particular intervention, but also identify what the next steps may be in increasing the evidence base of those services that anecdotally appear to be effective.

# DIFFERENTIATION BETWEEN EVIDENCE-BASED PRACTICES AND CLINICAL PRACTICE GUIDELINES

Clinical practice guidelines are developed from research findings or by consensus panels of experts in the field. They are intended to assist clinicians in making more informed decisions about how to treat individuals and families. Clinical guidelines and evidence-based practices share the same purpose: "to translate research into practice, increase the effectiveness of treatment, provide a framework for collecting data about treatment, ensure accountability to funding sources, and to encourage some consistency in practice." The primary difference between the two is that practice guidelines are developed by reviewing a broad spectrum of research literature to obtain a synthesized picture of what works. Evidence-based practices however, reflect one theoretical approach and provide detailed instructions for implementing that single approach to treatment (The Iowa consortium for substance abuse research and evaluation, 2003).

## GUIDING VALUES AND PRINCIPLES

The Department's philosophy regarding evidence-based practices, centers around four core values. These are:

1. Consumers and persons in recovery have the right to the highest quality and most effective treatment that is available at any given time.
2. Services should aid consumers in their recovery journey. As such, evidence based practices should not focus on the maintenance of illness, or simply symptom reduction, but rather the promotion of full, functional lives that foster independence and the attainment of personally meaningful goals such as employment, personal relationships and community integration.
3. Evidence based practices need to be culturally competent for the population being served. As such, programs may need to adjust practices to ensure that they are relevant, accessible, and effective for cultural groups that are different from the original study group in language and/or behavior.
4. Evidence based practices should not be chosen and implemented in a vacuum. Instead, providers should collaborate with consumers, family members and other stakeholders when selecting and implementing a practice.

## STRATEGIES FOR THE ADOPTION AND IMPLEMENTATION OF EVIDENCE-BASED PRACTICES

Research indicates that there are numerous factors that influence an organization's level of success in adopting and implementing an evidence based-practice. These include organizational readiness to adopt a new practice, the organizational infrastructure to support the implementation of the practice, the level of stakeholder buy-in, the level of commitment to devoting resources to the implementation process, attitudes and knowledge about research and the presence of practice-research partnerships (The Iowa Consortium for substance abuse research and evaluation, 2003).

## RECOMMENDATIONS FOR ACTION

The Philadelphia Behavioral Health System, with the support of the Department, is embarking on a systematic process to increasingly integrate EBP's into routine service delivery. It is not the expectation of the Department that providers select only practices that are supported by rigorous scientific evidence. Instead, the expectation is that providers articulate the type and level of evidence that supports the proposed practice. Additionally, the proposed evaluation of the program must be rigorous enough to assess not only the quality of services provided, but also the effectiveness of the services. The ability to monitor outcomes is one of the foundational components of implementing evidence-based practices. Program outcomes should be relevant and measurable. The more relevant the outcomes are to persons in recovery and to the organization, the more likely it is that the practice will be accepted by stakeholders (Rosswurm & Larrabee, 1999). Addressing the following issues will accomplish initial steps toward the goal of identifying and integrating EBPs into the Philadelphia behavioral health system of care.

1. Upon what level of evidence is the practice/program based?
2. What is the nature of that evidence and how was it obtained (e.g. scientific data, expert consensus in the literature, focus group data, program evaluation data, anecdotal positive treatment outcomes during previous implementations of the practice)?
3. Upon which population has the practice demonstrated effectiveness and is this comparable to the treatment population of your agency?
4. How is the practice likely to increase access to services, engagement and retention rates?
5. Can the practice be logistically applied in your setting?
6. Is the practice sufficiently operationalized for staff use? Are its key components clearly laid out?
7. What evidence do you have to suggest that the practice will be well accepted and supported by providers and persons in recovery?
8. How does the practice address cultural diversity and different populations? If the cultural relevance is insufficient, what process will be used to adapt the practice for the cultural groups served by your organization?
9. Can staff from a wide diversity of backgrounds and training use the practice?
10. What is the plan for continuing to build the level of evidence that supports its implementation with your population?

## References

Mary Ann Rosswurm, June H Larrabee Publication title: Image -- The Journal of Nursing Scholarship. Indianapolis: Fourth Quarter 1999. Vol. 31, Iss. 4; pg. 317, 6 pgs

## Resources

# Print Resources

Torrey, W. C., Finnerty, M., Evans A.C., and Wyzik, P (2003). Strategies for Leading the Implementation of Evidence-Based Practices. Psychiatric Clinics of North America

Drake, R.E., Goldman, H., Leff, S.H., Lehman, A. F., Dixon, L., Mueser, K.T., Torrey, W.C., Implementing Evidence-Based Practices in Routine Mental Health Service Settings. Psychiatric Services. 52, (2), February, 2001.

Evidence-Based Practices: An Implementation Guide for Community-Based Substance Abuse Treatment Agencies. The Iowa Practice Improvement Collaborative Project, Iowa Consortium for Substance Abuse Research and Evaluation at the University of Iowa, Spring, 2003.

Evidence-Based Mental Health Notebook. Teaching Evidence-Based Practice in Mental Health. 2, (3), August, 1999.

Freese, Frederick J. III, Stanley, J., Kress, K., and Vogel-Scibilia, S. Integrating Evidence-Based Practices and the Recovery Model, Psychiatric Services, 52, (11), November, 2001.

Geddes, J., Reynolds, S., Streiner, D., Szatmari, P., Evidence-Based Practice in Mental Health: New Journal Acknowledges an Approach Whose Time has Come (editorial). British Medical Journal, 315, (7121) p1483(2). Dec 6, 1997

Torrey, William C., Drake, R. E., Dixon, L., Burns, B. J., Flynn, L., Rush, J.A., Clark, R.E., Klatzker, D., Implementing Evidence-Based Practices for Persons With Severe Mental Illnesses. Psychiatric Services. 52, (1), January, 2001.

## Web Sites

Agency for Healthcare Quality and Research
http://mentalhealth.samhsa.gov/cmhs/communitysupport/toolkits/about.asp

Iowa Consortium for Mental Health
http://www.medicine.uiowa.edu/icmh/evidence/

NRI Center for Mental Health Quality and Accountability
http://nri.rdmc.org/CMHQA.cfm

National Association of State Program Mental Health Directors, Research Institute, Inc.
http://www.nri-inc.org

Northeast Addiction Transfer Technology Center
http://www.neattc.org/

New York State Office of Mental Health
http://www.omh.state.ny.us/omhweb/EBP/

Promising Practices Network on Children, Families and Communities
http://www.promisingpractices.net/

Substance Abuse and Mental Health Services Administration, National Mental Health Information Center
Toolkits:
Shaping MH Services Towards Recovery Evidence Based Practice Implementation Resource Kits: 1) Illness Management and Recovery, 2) Medication Management Approaches in Psychiatry, 3) ACT, 4) Family Psychoeducation, 5) Supported Employment, 6) Co-Occurring Disorders
http://mentalhealth.samhsa.gov/cmhs/communitysupport/toolkits/about.asp

The National Implementation Research Project at the University of South Florida
http://nirn.fmhi.usf.edu/

http://www.mhanys.org/ebpdb/

# Appendix D

# Trauma-informed Care: From Survival to Thriving

National leaders, including the Substance Abuse and Mental Health Services Administration, have been increasing their momentum toward a national understanding of the prevalence and effects of trauma and their implications for clinical and recovery support services.

Early and recent experiences of psychological trauma are common among people who seek mental health and substance use services. The spectrum of effects that these experiences leave behind can have profound effects on:

- people's vulnerability to the development of mental health and substance use challenges to which they are genetically predisposed;
- the course and complexity of physical, mental health and substance-related challenges;
- willingness to seek services and ability to overcome the obstacles to participation in services;
- psychological safety within service settings and vulnerability to retraumatization through traditional modes of treatment (e.g., seclusion, restraint, confrontive approaches);
- ability to participate safely and effectively in community-based recovery support structures; and
- vulnerability to recurrence of the symptoms of mental health and substance use challenges.

Providers can take a number of measures to create safety and healing for people who have experienced trauma. Principal among them are integrated services; respect; a focus on strengths and resilience factors; collaborative service relationships; giving people choices, control and opportunities for meaningful involvement and leadership; and attention to the family, the community and the culture—all essential elements of the emerging Philadelphia model.

Like the focus on resilience and recovery, the focus on trauma-informed care is aimed at promoting, not only the healing of wounds, but also the transformation of human lives, families and communities. If healing takes place in safe environments, people often do find that they are "stronger in the broken places"—and, in reality, not broken at all.

The confluence of all these national trends has directed a new level of energy, commitment and focus toward the transformation of behavioral health service systems across the nation. The recent healthcare reform measures have catapulted the sweeping rhetoric associated with system transformation into a national action agenda. Philadelphia is not only poised to meet the demands of this changing behavioral health landscape, but also uniquely positioned to help shape the nature of future behavioral health services.

# DBHIDS Guidelines and Staff Competencies for a Trauma-Informed System of Care

*The City of Philadelphia*
*Department of Behavioral Health and Intellectual disAbility Services*
*Trauma Task Force*

## Introduction

The Philadelphia Department of Behavioral Health and Intellectual disAbility Services (DBH/IDS) initiated the formation of a Trauma Task Force in November 2006 for the purpose of developing recommendations toward a trauma-informed system of care. Members of the task force were selected on the basis of their knowledge of trauma and its impact on the recovery and resilience of children, youth, adults and families, as well as their experience in working in this area from all perspectives. The impetus for the development of the Trauma Task Force was the result of the work being done as part of Systems Transformation and the Blue Ribbon Commission, now known as the Philadelphia COMPACT. It was evident through these efforts that there was a need for greater understanding within the provider community of the impact of all forms of trauma and traumatic loss—abuse, neglect, abandonment, death of parents, early childhood disrupted attachment experiences, sexual exploitation, domestic violence, community violence, war violence and gun violence. This area also includes trauma related to the loss of primary attachment that results when children are placed out of home during infancy or early childhood. Children often experience multiple foster placements or are institutionalized in settings that inadvertently re-traumatize them because of providers lack of knowledge in implementing trauma-informed interventions within a trauma-sensitive environment.

Research has clearly demonstrated that the majority of children and adults in behavioral health and social service systems have trauma histories. Adults with substance use challenges have trauma-related symptoms that inhibit their ability to attain and sustain recovery. Youth experiencing delinquency and individuals who are incarcerated have trauma histories that play a role in the development of their co-occurring mental health and substance use challenges as well as promoting criminal behavior. This increases the chances that people will enter the system multiple times. In order to adequately serve the needs of people receiving services, all health providers, including mental health and AOD (alcohol and other drug) treatment providers, and agencies providing services to people involved with the criminal justice system, must understand the complex and profound neurological, biological, psychological and emotional effects of trauma, traumatic loss and exposure to violence. Despite the fact that there is a large knowledge base about the profound impact of past trauma as well as extensive evidence for the necessity of providing trauma-informed care, there is still a lack of proper assessment for histories in our human service sector. In addition, there exists a lack of understanding about the impact of trauma which affects symptom presentation, treatment participation and outcome, and a lack of knowledge of trauma-specific treatment and trauma-informed care that often results in retraumatization.

Being trauma informed includes a provider's understanding of the prevalence of trauma, the recognition of primary and secondary diagnoses related to trauma, and the recognition of culture and practices that are re-traumatizing. The assessment process for any level of care must include the assessment of trauma histories and symptoms. More important, staff must understand the function of behavior such as rage, oppositional behaviors, self-harm, obsessive/compulsive behaviors, etc.

that relates to respective trauma histories of people seeking services. The lack of understanding and recognition leads to inappropriate diagnoses (or over-diagnosing disorders such as schizophrenia, bipolar, oppositional/defiant or conduct disorder in children and youth, etc.), misinterpretation of behaviors that may result in coercive and overpowering approaches to treatment, and, ultimately, to more harm being done.

As the system moves more towards transformation of its services to promote recovery and resilience, the issue of trauma has to be addressed at the level of organizational commitment to becoming trauma-informed and at the level of ensuring staff competencies to provide trauma-specific treatment. Being trauma-informed includes leadership and administrative commitment to trauma-informed change that encompasses:

a. Provision of trauma training to all staff including administrative and support personnel.

b. Incorporating trauma-related concerns into the interviewing and hiring process to ensure that staff recruitment is based upon the attached staff competencies.

c. The incorporation of people with lived experience (trauma survivors) into designing and evaluation of services. These need to be people who have achieved enough recovery to be able to work on the task rather than impose their own personal agendas or (even more important) their their own unfinished business onto the task, e.g. people in recovery who are not dealing with severe boundary, grief, or other issues within the task force, but who can separate these issues out and bring them up in a constructive way when they are relevant.

d. Review and development of formal and informal policies and procedures to ensure they reflect a thorough understanding of trauma and the needs of trauma survivors.

e. A thorough understanding of the ways in which acute and chronic organizational stress and chronic discord within an organization can adversely affect proper service delivery to people receiving services who have been traumatized.

Trauma-specific services are those that are designed to treat the symptoms associated with trauma. These include grounding techniques which help manage dissociative symptoms, cognitive behavioral therapy, desensitization therapies which help individuals to manage their painful memories (body, visual, tactile memories associated with the actual traumatic event), and behavioral and other therapies which help individuals modulate their emotional responses and work through loss.

The Department of Behavioral Health and Intellectual disAbility Services, through the work of the Trauma Task Force, has created requirements and expectations for all behavioral health providers who provide the range of trauma services to children, youth and adults. These requirements and expectations are based upon those elements developed by the Substance Abuse and Mental Health Services Administration which are necessary to create a trauma-informed system of care for vulnerable children and adults. These requirements will be:

1. Included in any RFP/RFI/RFA/RFQ issued by DBH/IDS for new, enhanced or expanded services.

2. Incorporated into the review of any program requests or requests that are issued by DBH/IDS to develop any level of care or service.

3. Integrated into the credentialing and recredentialing of providers and in the monitoring process.

4. Used to assess current self-identified trauma-treatment specific providers to ensure they meet the definition of trauma informed and meet the staff competency requirements for providing that treatment.

## Requirements for Trauma-Specific Treatment Services

DBH/IDS providers who offer specialized trauma-specific treatment, or who are requesting to provide trauma services, must meet the following conditions to qualify under the definition of being trauma-informed:

1. Incorporate trauma into their mission statement.

2. Conduct trauma screenings and assessments.

3. Adhere to trauma-informed clinical practice guidelines and treatment approaches.

4. Ensure that specialized trauma programs integrate both mental health and substance use services.

5. Identify in their respective policy and procedure manual procedures ways of avoiding retraumatization of people receiving services and of staff.

6. Provide staff training, and develop recruitment standards and job qualifications that meet the competencies required to provide trauma-specific treatment.

7. Include people receiving services, their families and other supporters, survivors and other recovering persons at all levels of planning, development, and implementation of services.

8. Have trauma policies and services that respect culture, nationality, ethnicity, gender, gender identity or expression, age, sexual orientation, and physical disability.

9. Demonstrate through policies and procedures as well as clinical documentation that they have a trauma-informed organizational culture that prioritizes the importance of maintaining the physical, psychological, social and moral safety and well-being of people receiving services and staff

10. Demonstrate through CQI or similar documentation that trauma procedures, training, hiring, and the above criteria have actually been implemented and are being followed.

Providers must demonstrate that trauma-specific treatment includes the following elements:

1. **Assessment and evaluation:** All assessments and/or comprehensive biopsychosocial evaluations must include evidence that staff obtained trauma histories and are aware of assessment protocols for different situations and groups of people receiving services. Standardized trauma assessment tools should be incorporated into the evaluation process.

2. **Trauma-specific treatment services**: Providers must demonstrate that the services are designed to treat the actual sequelae of sexual, emotional, physical, community, natural disaster, terrorism or war trauma. Techniques

such as "grounding,"desensitization therapies, behavioral therapies, or other "best practice models" or evidence-supported/based models of therapy, as determined by organizations such as the National Child Traumatic Stress Network, the International Society for Traumatic Stress Studies, The International Society for the Study of Dissociation, National Coalition Against Domestic Violence, etc. are examples of such treatment interventions.

3. **Staff training and supervision**: Providers must demonstrate evidence of trauma-informed staff training about trauma and violence issues, and how to provide treatment and care to individuals within their specific service settings who have experienced trauma or violence. Evidence must include the background and experience of the trainers and evidence of on-going case supervision and consultation.

4. Trauma-Informed Staff Competencies: In addition to trauma-specific treatment services, providers must show evidence that staff providing trauma-specific treatment have trauma-based competencies as follows:

   a. **Characteristics and Terminology**: Staff must understand terminology used to distinguish different types of abuse and trauma, e.g. sexual abuse, domestic violence, neglect, experiences of war, natural disaster, terrorism, etc.

   b. Impact: Staff must have knowledge that trauma and abuse have many facets and how these experiences can affect human development and functioning. It is also important for staff to understand and define traumatic stress responses such as: psychological arousal, intrusive recollections, numbing/avoidance, and other stress responses.

   c. Effects in Different Population Groups: Staff must have knowledge of how trauma affects different types of individuals, particularly those with mental health issues, intellectual disabilities, and those who are using substances. This also includes a basic understanding of possible gender-related effects of trauma, as well as race-related and LGBT-related effects of trauma.

   d. Understanding of trauma as it relates to cultural backgrounds: Staff must have an understanding of the impact of trauma on different cultures particularly as it relates to attitudes, meaning of abuse, and other cultural factors that may impede accessing treatment. and Culture-Bound Syndromes of *amok, ataque de Nervios, falling out or blacking out, latah, nervios, pibloktoq, qi-gong psychotic reaction, shin-byung, spell, susto,* and *zar* that are often seen as being dissociative symptoms,

   e. **Assessment Options, Approaches and Tools**: Staff must be able to obtain trauma history in their assessments and be aware of assessment protocols for different situations and client groups.

   f. Attitudes and Values: Staff must have an understanding of the history and context of attitudes toward abuse and abuse survivors in mental health and other settings. This includes the theoretical frameworks of behavioral health diagnosis and treatment.

   g. **Stages of and Key Elements in Recovery**: Staff must be able to cite at least two (2) different frameworks for understanding the process of and goals for recovery from trauma. This includes the ability to utilize approaches to address psychological trauma and to communicate to people receiving services the basic tools for managing and coping with the effects of traumatic stress, e.g. grounding, reality checking, feelings checking, imagery, journal writing, artwork, talking.

h. **Vicarious Trauma, Parallel Process, and Organizational Stress**. Administrators and staff must have a working knowledge and participate in regular forums for understanding the ways in which helping people recover from trauma may impact their own lives, the way they behave toward each other, and ultimately may determine whether or not proper care is delivered to people receiving services. The organization must be able to demonstrate positive ways to cope with the chronic and acute stressors associated with service delivery that demonstrate sensitivity to the well-being of staff, enhances service delivery and prevent the development of destructive parallel processes within the organization.

i. Trauma and Youth: Traumatic experiences for youth can include physical or sexual abuse or assault but also serious accidents, illnesses, disasters and the loss of important relationships. Early trauma affects brain and personality development, and may inhibit one's ability to self-regulate. Trauma involving victimization is more likely to lead to impairment in psychosocial functioning and physical health (Kessler, R.C., Sonnega, A., Bromte, E. Hughes, M. & Nelson, C.B.-1995).

j. Trauma and Delinquency: Because behaviors associated with trauma often look very similar to common delinquent behaviors, staff must understand the multiple pathways to similar symptom patterns (Ford, J.D. (2002): Traumatic Victimization in Childhood and Persistent Problems with Oppositional Defiance).

5. **People with Lived Experience:** For many people, trauma-informed services address - sometimes for the first time - the problem *underlying* their symptoms. This can be critical for recovery. In addition, inquiring about, recognizing, and acknowledging trauma gives people an opportunity to talk about "what happened to them" rather than "what's wrong with them" – immediately making it possible for healing to begin.[1]

# TRAUMA-SPECIFIC TREATMENT COMPETENCY COMPONENTS

The following are defined competencies recommended by the Philadelphia Trauma Task Force that should be incorporated into any RFP process or request by a provider that is seeking to develop, enhance or expand trauma-specific treatment services

1. **Characteristics and Terminology:**

   a. Staff must know differences between trauma-specific services and trauma-informed system of care.

   b. Staff understands that trauma-specific services are designed to treat symptoms associated with trauma. These services include, for example, grounding techniques, which help manage dissociative symptoms, cognitive behavioral therapy, desensitization therapies which help individuals to manage their painful memories (body, visual, tactile memories associated with the actual traumatic event), and behavioral therapies which help individuals modulate their emotional responses.

   c. Staff understands key principles of trauma-informed services; ensuring physical and emotional safety; maximizing person-directed choice and control; maintaining clarity of tasks and boundaries; ensuring collaboration in the sharing of power; maximizing empowerment and skill building.

d. Staff can distinguish different types of abuse and trauma; e.g. sexual abuse, domestic violence, neglect, community violence, experiences of war, natural disaster, etc. This includes understanding what makes an event, relationship, or situation traumatic as opposed to problematic.

e. Staff must have knowledge of existing standardized trauma-specific screening and assessment instruments. Two examples include the Posttraumatic Stress Diagnostic Scale (PSD; Foa, 1995) and the Trauma Symptom Inventory (TSI; Briere, 1995). The PSD is a 49-item instrument that determines the diagnosis of PTSD. The TSI consists of 100 items that measure posttraumatic stress and other trauma-related symptoms (e.g., depression, anger/irritability, sexual concerns).

2. **Impact**

a. Staff must have knowledge about the many faces of trauma and abuse and how they can affect human development.

b. Staff must have knowledge of stress responses such as psychological arousal, intrusive recollections, numbing, avoidance, and other stress responses.

c. Staff must have knowledge of and be able to assess secondary victimization, which consists of identifying interactions with community systems, exploring exposure to victim-blaming attitudes, behaviors; and practices; and determining impact on the survivor.

d. Staff must have knowledge of the cluster of symptoms, adaptations, and reactions that interfere with the functioning of an individual who has been victimized by severe physical abuse and injury, sexual abuse and/ or exploitation, witnessing or surviving severe community or domestic violence (including accidents, natural or human-caused disasters) and post-war PTSD symptoms.

e. Staff is familiar with current research on the prevalence of psychological (childhood and adult) trauma in the lives of persons with serious mental health and substance use challenges and is able to list possible sequelae of trauma (e.g. post traumatic stress disorder (PTSD), depression, generalized anxiety, self-injury, substance use, flashbacks, dissociation, eating disorder, revictimization, physical illness, suicide, aggression toward others).

f. Staff must be aware of the emotional, physical, cognitive and behavioral symptoms of individuals who experience traumatic events.

3. **Effects in Different Populations/Groups:**

a. Staff must have knowledge about ways in which patterns of responses to the environment are determined by unique personal beliefs, perceptions, assumptions, and interpretations across different cultural groups

b. Staff must have knowledge of how trauma affects different types of individuals, particularly those with mental health issues, intellectual disabilities, and those who are using substances. This also includes a basic understanding of possible gender-related effects of trauma.

c. Staff must have an understanding of the impact of trauma on different cultures particularly as it relates to attitudes, meaning of abuse, and other cultural factors that may impede accessing treatment. Cultural values play an important role in making sense of that trauma within a certain culture.

d. Staff must understand how trauma resonates deeply with a public traumatized by terrorism and aware of the effects of PTSD and other trauma-induced conditions on veterans, political refugees, and people who have experienced war and natural disasters.

4. **Assessment Options, Approaches and Tools:**

a. Staff must be able to obtain trauma history in their assessments and be aware of assessment protocols for different situations and groups of people.

b. Staff must have knowledge of assessment instruments including Trauma Exposure measures, Adult PTSD Self-Report Measures, Adult PTSD Interviews, Child Measures, etc. Examples of other measures include:

- Dimensions of Stressful Events (DOSE)
- Traumatic Events Screening Inventory*(TESI)
- Childhood PTSD Interview
- Children's Posttraumatic Stress Disorder Inventory (CPTSDI)
- Clinician-Administered PTSD Scale for Children & Adolescents (CAPS-CA)
- My Worst Experiences Survey
- UCLA PTSD Index for DSM-IV
- When Bad Things Happen Scale (WBTH)
- Child PTSD Reaction Index*(CPTS-RI)
- Child PTSD Symptom Scale
- Children's Impact of Traumatic Events Scale-Revised (CITES-2)
- CPTS-RI Revision 2 (aka PTSD Index for DSM-IV)
- Parent Report of Child's Reaction to Stress
- Trauma Symptom Checklist for Children (TSCC)
- Trauma Symptom Checklist for Young Children (TSCYC)

c. Staff must have an understanding of different behavioral interventions that encompass stress management, muscle relaxation and breathing techniques, thought stopping and thought replacement.

d. Staff must understand the key areas of assessing issues such as cultural identity, trans-generational experiences, cultural values, beliefs about the presenting problem, attitudes and expectations related to therapy, attitudinal barriers, and discrimination experiences.

e. Staff working with youth who may be delinquent must be trained in screening instruments used to screen for trauma exposure and traumatic stress among youth in the juvenile justice or child welfare system:

   1. **MAYSI-2** – This is a mental health-screening instrument frequently used in juvenile justice programs. It is a 52-item self-report instrument that includes a Traumatic Experiences Scale.

   2. **Traumatic Events Screening Inventory (TESI):** This is a structured clinical interview that briefly assesses a youth, parent or guardian's report of the youth's past or current exposure to a range of traumatic events.

   3. **PTSD Reaction Index (PTSD-RI):** This is a self-report symptom inventory based closely on the DSM-IV criteria for post-traumatic stress disorder. Twenty of the items assess PTSD symptoms and two items assess the associated features of fear of re-occurrence and guilt.

   4. **Trauma Symptom Checklist for Children (TSCC):** This is a 54-item self-report symptom inventory made up of six scales and four subscales designed to evaluate acute and chronic traumatic stress symptoms.

   5. **PTSD Checklist for Children/Parent Report (PCL-C/PR):** This is a brief measure of PTSD symptom severity completed by parent or other adults who have daily contact with the youth (probation staff, social workers, treatment foster or general foster care parents, etc.).

## Attitudes and Values:

a. Staff must have an understanding of the history and context of attitudes toward abuse and abuse survivors in mental health and other settings. This includes the theoretical frameworks of behavioral health diagnosis and treatment.

b. Staff must address the most fundamental operating principle of medical and human services: "Do no harm."

c. Staff must understand the difference in experiences of trauma as it relates to different cultural groups including understanding a person's acculturation and being able to explore their experiences through their own eyes.

d. Staff must understand the need for and particular elements of "empowerment" for trauma survivors and that people with the lived experience of trauma need to be full partners in all recovery planning, development and evaluation.

## Stages of and Key Elements in Recovery:

a. Staff is able to cite at least two (2) different frameworks for understanding the process of and goals for recovery from trauma.

b. Staff must have an understanding of how to address approaches to addressing psychological trauma and to communicate to people receiving services basic tools for managing and coping with the effects of traumatic stress, e.g. grounding, reality checking, feelings checking, imagery, journal writing, artwork, talking.

c. Staff must value and have an understanding or awareness of people with lived experience that represent the "Voices" of trauma – individuals talking about their personal journey.

# Appendix E

# Diversity of Strengths

The diversity of strengths that can serve as resources for the person and his or her recovery planning team is respected. Saleeby (2001), for example, recommended conceptualizing strengths broadly to include the following dimensions:

a. Skills (e.g., gardening, caring for children, speaking Spanish, doing budgets);

b. Talents (e.g., playing the bagpipes, cooking);

c. Personal virtues and traits (e.g., insight, patience, sense of humor, self-discipline);

d. Interpersonal skills (e.g., comforting others, giving advice, mediating conflicts);

e. Interpersonal and environmental resources (e.g., extended family, good neighbors);

f. Cultural knowledge and lore (e.g., healing ceremonies and rituals, stories of cultural perseverance);

g. Family stories and narratives (e.g., migration and settlement, falls from grace and then redemption);  (Copeland)

h. Knowledge gained from struggling with adversity (e.g., how one came to survive past events, how one maintains hope and faith);

i. Knowledge gained from occupational or parental roles (e.g., caring for others, planning events);

j. Spirituality and faith (e.g., a system of meaning to rely on, a declaration of purpose beyond self); and

k. Hopes and dreams (e.g., personal goals and vision, positive expectations about a better future).

## Appendix F

# Areas of Inquiry When Conducting a Person-first Assessment

- Personal Strengths: e.g., What are you most proud of in your life? What is one thing you would not change about yourself?
- Interests and Activities: e.g., If you could plan the "perfect day," what would it look like?
- Cultural Identity: e.g., How do you identify yourself culturally? Which aspects of your cultural identity are most important or meaningful to you (race, ethnicity, gender, sexual orientation, spirituality, values)?
- Living Environment: e.g., What are the most important things to you when deciding where to live?
- Employment: e.g., What would be your ideal job?
- Learning: e.g., What kinds of things have you liked learning about in the past?
- Trauma: e.g., Have there been people in your life who have hurt you in some way in the past (physically, emotionally, sexually)? In relationships with other previous or current therapist(s) and/or doctor(s), have you ever been treated inappropriately or in ways that were harmful to you (e.g., poor boundaries, sexual inappropriateness, physical abuse, etc.)?
- Safety and Legal Issues: e.g., Do you have any legal issues that are causing you problems?
- Financial: e.g., Would you like to be more independent with managing your finances? If so, how do you think you could do that?
- Lifestyle and Health: e.g., Do you have any concerns about your overall health? What are those concerns? What does a good day look like? A bad day?
- Choice Making: e.g., What are the some of the choices that you currently make in your life? Are there choices in your life that are made for you?
- Transportation: e.g., How do you currently get around from place to place? What would help?
- Faith and Spirituality: e.g., What type of spiritual or faith activities do you participate in? Is faith or spirituality important to you? Are there spiritual leaders, healers, shamans to whom you turn for support and/or guidance?
- Relationships and Important People: e.g., Who is the person in your life who believes in you? In what ways does this person convey this belief in you?
- Hopes and Dreams: e.g., Tell me a bit about your hopes or dreams for the future.   (Tondora, 2005).

# Appendix G

# DBHIDS Policy on Services to LGBTQI People

All employees of any facility contracting with DBHIDS to provide substance use treatment and/or mental health services must demonstrate an awareness of and commitment to providing affirmative services for people who identify as Lesbian, Gay, Bisexual, Transgender, Queer/Questioning or Intersex (LGBTQI) receiving mental health and/or substance use services, which includes, but is not limited to:

- An awareness of one's own attitudes, beliefs, and biases about LGBTQI people and the effect that these might have on LGBTQI people (people who receive services, their families or other supports, staff, visitors) with whom one is working

- An awareness of any changes in one's own perspective that might be needed in order to ensure a welcoming and affirming climate for LGBTQI people (including people who receive services, their families or other supports, staff, and visitors) in the facility

- An awareness of the effects of discrimination, bias, prejudice, stigma, and acts of hate on the lives and mental health of LGBTQI people

- An awareness of preferred and potentially problematic terminology pertaining to sexual orientation, gender variance, and gender identity

- An awareness of the policy statements of major medical and mental health associations pertaining to working with LGBTQI people

- An awareness of the policy statements of DBHIDS, behavioral health managed care organizations, and the provider regarding working with LGBTQI people

- An awareness of local, state, and national legislation affecting LGBTQI people

- An awareness that sexual orientation and gender identity/variance are often not immediately evident and of the importance of not making assumptions

- An understanding that homophobia and transphobia are issues as significant as racism, classism and sexism and that these issues are to be addressed without re-victimization.

- An understanding that sexual orientation and gender identity are not mental health issues albeit some folks who are LGBTQI may experience mental health and or substance use challenges that can be related to their experiences of homophobia and or transphobia as well as racism, classism and sexism.

In addition to the demonstrated awareness expected of all employees, all clinical staff, both professional and paraprofessional, of any facility contracting with DBHIDS to provide substance use and/or mental health services must demonstrate knowledge and understanding of the life experiences of LGBTQI people and issues and concerns facing them as they seek mental health and/or substance use services, including, but not limited to:

- The difference between sexual orientation and gender identity

- Identity development as a sexual minority and/or gender variant individual
- Ways in which sexual orientation and/or gender identity/expression can interact with development across the lifespan
- The interaction of sexual orientation and gender identity/expression with other personal characteristics and social locations such as race, ethnicity, nationality, socio-economic class, religious/spiritual affiliation and practices, ability/disability, age, geographic location, etc.
- The relationships that LGBTQI people have with others in their lives, including intimate relationships, parenting relationships, relationships with families of origin, relationships with families of choice
- The mental health consequences of stigma, discrimination, and prejudice on LGBTQI people
- Ways in which LGBTQI people can be resilient in the face of stigma, discrimination, and prejudice
- Local, state, and national resources to support LGBTQI people
- Ways in which to advocate on behalf of LGBTQI people

It is required that regular training and skills-building opportunities, conducted by specialists who work with people in LGBTQI communities, be a part of the staff development program for all agencies. Other requirements include:

- Two annual 6-hour training days that address meeting the clinical needs of LGBQ as well as transgender, gender non-conforming and individuals who are intersex
- Professional involvement with groups that support LGBTQI people
- All facilities contracting with DBHIDS to provide substance use and/or mental health services have at least one master's-level clinician on staff who specializes in providing services to LGBTQI people

Facilities providing services funded by DBHIDS will ensure a welcoming and affirming environment for LGBTQI people receiving services, their families and other supporters, staff, and visitors. Efforts to ensure such an environment shall include, but not be limited to:

- Including statements on actual or perceived sexual orientation and actual or perceived gender identity and gender expression in their non-discrimination policies
- Using language that is inclusive of all sexual orientations and gender identities on all forms and paperwork
- Providing a physical environment that expresses inclusion of sexual minority and gender non-conforming individuals (e.g., periodicals of particular interest to these populations, pictures that portray diversity with respect to sexual orientation and gender identity)
- Providing some bathrooms that are not gender-specific
- Residential facilities for youths and adults must provide a mechanism to accommodate the needs for housing, programming, and or milieu that is appropriate and safe for transgender and gender non-conforming individuals
- In policy and practice, immediately and decisively addressing any hate speech or acts of intolerance on the part of other people receiving services, their families or other supporters, staff, or visitors

- Promoting people receiving services identifying whom to consider family with respect to participation in family programs
- Ensuring that any programs or facilities to which people are referred have policies and practices that are affirming to sexual minorities and gender non-conforming people
- Providing necessary documentation that supports transgender adults and youth who are seeking gender alignment services as long as it is clinically appropriate, until such documentation is no longer required

The following documents developed and adopted by major medical and mental health associations were used in developing this policy. DBHIDS recognizes and endorses these documents as representing best practice in working with LGBTQI people:

Substance Abuse and Mental Health Services Administration: Center for Substance Abuse Treatment

*A Provider's Introduction to Substance Abuse Treatment for Lesbian, Gay, Bisexual, and Transgender Individuals*

American Psychological Association

*Guidelines for Psychotherapy with Lesbian, Gay, and Bisexual Clients*

*Report of the APA Task Force on Gender Identity and Gender Variance*

Report of the APA Task Force on Appropriate Therapeutic Responses to Sexual Orientation

Appropriate Therapeutic Responses to Sexual Orientation

Resolution on Appropriate Affirmative Responses to Sexual Orientation Distress and Change Efforts

APA Policy Statement: Transgender, Gender Identity, & Gender Expression Non-Discrimination

American Counseling Association/Association for Lesbian, Gay, Bisexual, and Transgender Issues in Counseling

*Competencies for Counseling Gay, Lesbian, Bisexual Clients*

Competencies for Counseling Transgender Clients

Ethical Issues Related to Conversion or Reparative Therapy

World Professional Association for Transgender Health (WPATH)

The Harry Benjamin International Gender Dysphoria Association's Standards of Care for Gender Identity Disorders, Sixth Version (2001

American Academy of Pediatrics

*Clinical Report: Sexual Orientation and Adolescents*

Gay and Lesbian Medical Association

*Guidelines for Care of Lesbian, Gay, Bisexual, and Transgender Patients*

*Healthy People 2010: Companion Document for Lesbian, Gay, Bisexual, and Transgender (LGBT) Health*

National Association of Social Workers

Policy Statement on Practice Standards for clients who are LGBT (2005)

*"Reparative" and "Conversion" Therapies for Lesbians and Gay Men: Position Statement by National Committee on Lesbian, Gay, and Bisexual Issues, NASW*

American School Counseling Association

# Appendix H

# Blue Ribbon Commission Goals and Recommendations

**From the Final Report of the Mayor's Blue Ribbon Commission on Children's Behavioral Health, City of Philadelphia**

January, 2007

Goal 1: Children's Social and Emotional Well-Being Is the Responsibility of the Entire Community

**Recommendation 1.1**
Advance a framework of resiliency based on the strengths of children and their families throughout the community.

**Recommendation 1.2**
Support parents and caregivers in their emotional attachment and bonding to children and youth.

**Recommendation 1.3**
Create community strategies to build public awareness and knowledge of factors that promote social and emotional health and safety.

**Recommendation 1.4**
Develop strategies to strengthen communities and address environmental factors affecting social and emotional health and safety.

**Recommendation 1.5**
Ensure that all agencies and organizations commit to promoting the behavioral health of the children they serve.

Goal 2: Every Child and Family Served by the Behavioral Health System, or Other

Service Systems, Is Valued and Treated With Dignity and Respect

**Recommendation 2.1**
Create opportunities in child-serving systems for children and families to have a voice in decision-making regarding planning, service delivery and treatment.

**Recommendation 2.2**
Deliver services and supports in a way that respects and is responsive to children's racial, ethnic, and cultural backgrounds, sexual orientation, and gender identities.

**Recommendation 2.3**
Create mechanisms for a youth and family peer component to be integrated into all behavioral health care services for children and youth, and place peer support in communities with children and families.

## Goal 3: Prevention, Early Identification, and Early Intervention Activities Help Children and Their Families to Prevent Behavioral Health Problems, or Reduce Their Impact Once They Arise

### Recommendation 3.1
Improve and expand broad-based prevention and health promotion activities to keep all children on the right track.

### Recommendation 3.2
Identify and intervene early with children who are vulnerable to behavioral health problems.

### Recommendation 3.3
Identify, promptly refer, and secure services for children and youth experiencing behavioral health problems, including those in early care and education, school settings, and the child welfare and juvenile justice systems.

## Goal 4: Children and Families Are Able to Obtain Quality Services When and Where They Need Them

### Recommendation 4.1
Provide children and families with information about all available services.

### Recommendation 4.2
Develop better access points to services and supports for children and their families.

### Recommendation 4.3
Ensure availability of a full array of quality, culturally competent and community based services for children and their families.

### Recommendation 4.4
Make every effort to move children from distant and residential settings to community and home settings.

## Goal 5: Supports and Services for Children and Families Are Effective and Provided by Skilled and Knowledgeable Providers and Staff

### Recommendation 5.1
Create and employ accountability and quality assurance measures to ensure effective services.

### Recommendation 5.2
Expand the number of professionals and paraprofessionals serving children and families at all levels of care by developing strategies for recruiting, retaining and rewarding a skilled and culturally competent workforce.

### Recommendation 5.3
Upgrade the skills of those working with children by expanding and improving training and education for behavioral health and other staff.

### Recommendation 5.4
Boost the effectiveness of services by incorporating culturally sensitive, developmentally appropriate and trauma informed practices.

**Goal 6: True Collaboration Is Achieved at the Service Level and the System Level**

**Recommendation 6.1**
Improve coordination and integration across individual, service provider and system levels.

**Recommendation 6.2**
Develop specific reforms to improve collaboration in schools and between schools and the behavioral health system

**Recommendation 6.3**
Increase the integration of behavioral health and physical health services.

# Appendix I

# Family Resource Network Family Involvement Best Practice Guidelines

### Department of Behavioral Health and Intellectual disABILITY Services

### Family Resource Network Best Practice Guidelines Involving "Significant People," (SP) Identified by People Receiving Services In Behavioral Health Programs

## 1. ASSISTING PEOPLE RECEIVING SERVICES WITH IDENTIFYING SIGNIFICANT PEOPLE IN THEIR LIVES AND GIVING PERMISSION TO CONTACT SPs WHO ARE IMPORTANT TO THEIR RECOVERY.

During the intake process or soon after, **all people receiving services are encouraged by staff members to identify and provide "family friendly" signed releases for SPs who may have a positive or negative impact on their recovery.** Staff members also assist the person with identifying people who may help or hinder their recovery.

After regular clinical staff (for example, therapists and case managers) are assigned to a person, these staff members continue to make efforts to help people identify those who can be significant to their recovery, as well as continuing to make efforts to obtain permission to talk to family members and other SPs. This is *not* a one-shot, "mention once at intake" process.

## 2. INITIAL CONTACTS WITH SPS

Assigned staff members continue the collaborative process of identifying important SPs, and **with the approval of the person receiving services, contact them by phone as soon as possible to answer questions, seek information, and ask for their involvement and support in the person's recovery**.

There is special emphasis on clinicians contacting significant people by phone due to the difficulty many family members and other SPs have in making a workday trip to the clinician's office—especially if reliable transportation is not available, the SP has few financial resources, and/or has difficulty getting time off from his/her work.

A primary purpose for the initial phone call is to ask significant people about their concerns, to offer information about the agency and its programs, to offer information about sources of family support and education, and to ask for support in assisting the person in his/her recovery.

The assigned staff should also ask for any critical information on a person's strengths and capacities, past treatment successes and challenges that may be vital to his/her recovery.

The inability or unwillingness of family members or other SPs to travel to the agency site for personal interviews is *never* a reason for the absence of family contacts or continued outreach.

**NOTE**: The listing of "emergency contacts" for people receiving services is **not** "family involvement" unless those contacts are called routinely and not just in emergencies. "Emergency contacts" are by definition only for emergencies, and are usually not for helping people in their recovery. Lists of emergency contacts are not lists of SPs.

3. **INCLUDING SPS IN RECOVERY PLANNING**

   **Provider clinicians include appropriate family members and other significant people in agency team meetings with the person receiving services to discuss their recovery planning and encourage their ongoing efforts to help the person meet recovery goals.**

   As approved by the person receiving services, assigned clinicians make the earliest possible arrangements for family members and other SPs to be included in as many agency team recovery and continuing care planning meetings with the person and his or her team as possible.

   Families and other SPs are included in making contingency plans and other planning meetings that may have an impact on SPs and call for their understanding and/or cooperation. With permission of the person receiving services, results of such meetings should be communicated to SPs who couldn't attend but are a vital part of the person's recovery. **This is especially important when changes in service such as discharges or transfers are planned.**

4. **RESOURCES FOR SIGNIFICANT PEOPLE**

   **Provider staff members offer ongoing support and educational resources or referrals to families and other involved SPs (as opposed to family therapy).**

   This may include discussions of the person's diagnosis (with permission of the person) and the implications for recovery.

   The staff offers families written materials concerning family resources (including the FRN Family Resources Packet) as well as other up-to-date information.

5. **DOCUMENTATION**

   **Provider clinicians document all steps taken regarding SPs in clinical progress notes.**

   Documentation includes releases, efforts to obtain releases, staff contacts of any kind with SPs, and joint plans with the person receiving services and staff for future and ongoing involvement of SPs. Documentation includes explanations of why there is no staff contact with any SP, if that is the case. Documentation includes timely updates and descriptions of efforts involving SPs in the progress notes. The documentation provides enough detail to allow quality of care reviewers to judge the quality and amount of SP-related effort.

6. **QUALITY ASSURANCE/QUALITY IMPROVEMENT (QA/QI)**

   **Provider agencies routinely review documentation of the inclusion and support of significant people in the life of the person receiving services as part of their continuing QA/QI efforts.**

   Providers routinely review at least a sample of randomly-chosen records looking for evidence of documentation of all staff practices listed above, including identification of SPs and the proactive and timely outreach to all SPs with releases in all agency programs. Program staff members are made aware of strengths and challenges of the documentation in a timely fashion, and any challenges are addressed promptly and results/improvements documented.

Providers have regular meetings that include administrative level staff to review the overall effectiveness of family involvement efforts, and to plan and implement improvements.

Providers regularly survey at least a sample of people receiving services, staff members, and significant people and ask them about their awareness of specific practices occurring ( e.g., To an SP: "Did a staff member call you within two weeks of your family member being admitted to the day program?"), and their level of satisfaction with FI practices and policies. Since most people in human services surveys report high levels of satisfaction no matter what, satisfaction surveys are **not** a substitute for finding out what practices are actually occurring. Satisfaction surveys are developed either by people receiving services and their SPs or with their significant input into their design.

## 7. TRAINING AND SUPERVISION

**All therapists, case managers, and other assigned clinicians who work with significant people of those receiving services have had adequate training and experience, and receive ongoing clinical supervision.** Clinicians have at least one year of supervised family/SP liaison work, or they have received training in outreach to SPs (especially family members), engaging SPs in support of the person's recovery efforts, and knowing of and offering resources for SPs (especially families), and clinicians have demonstrated competence in these areas.

All clinicians working with families and SPs receive at least monthly ongoing clinical supervision that includes discussions of SP involvement and support issues.

## 8. INFORMING SIGNIFICANT PEOPLE OF AGENCY AND PROGRAM SERVICES

**Provider staff familiarize SPs with agency and program services** through conversations (asking for any questions that SPs may have) and literature. SPs are informed of the procedure for appealing decisions with which they disagree. SPs are informed of the names of program administrators. Any students or others in training inform SPs of their student status and the name of their supervisor (as required by professional ethics).

## 9. SP INPUT & INVOLVEMENT IN PROGRAM & POLICY DECISIONS

Staff proactively recruit family representatives to serve on agency boards of directors, policy or feedback committees, and to participate in QA/QI interviews and surveys.

# Appendix J

# Person-first Best Practice Guidelines

**Standard 1**
Philadelphia's health care departments, managed care organization, and provider organizations should ensure that people coming for services receive from all department and provider organization staff members effective, understandable, recovery-oriented and respectful care that is provided to ensure dignity and in a person-first manner compatible with their individual needs (race, ethnicity, language, gender, sexual orientation, social role, physical health challenges, elder status, etc.), health and recovery beliefs and practices and preferred language. Clergy/Indigenous healers are part of the process if requested by the person coming for services.

**Standard 2**
Philadelphia's health care departments, managed care organization, and provider organizations should implement strategies to recruit, retain, and promote at all levels of the organization a diverse staff and leadership that are representative of the demographic characteristics of the service area.

All marketing that is done in Philadelphia's communities should be created to respond to the needs of those communities.

**Standard 3**
Philadelphia's health care departments, managed care organization, and provider organizations should ensure that staff at all levels and across all disciplines receive ongoing education and training in recovery oriented systems of care, and service delivery that is person-first and responsive to the needs of Philadelphia's residents (see Standard I for definition).

**Standard 4**
Philadelphia's health care departments, managed care organization, and provider organizations must offer and provide language assistance services, including bilingual staff and interpreter services, at no cost to each person who comes for services and who possess limited English proficiency at all points of contact, in a timely manner during all hours of operation.

**Standard 5**
Philadelphia's health care departments, managed care organization, and provider organizations must provide people who come for services, in their preferred language, both verbal offers and written notices informing them of their right to receive language assistance services.

**Standard 6**
Philadelphia's health care departments, managed care organization, and provider organizations must assure the competence of language assistance provided to limited English proficient people who come for services by interpreters and bilingual

staff. Family and friends should not be used to provide interpretation services (except on request by the person receiving services).

**Standard 7**
Philadelphia's health care departments, managed care organization, and provider organizations must make available easily understood service-related materials and post signage in the languages of the commonly encountered groups and/or groups represented in the community in which the service is located.

**Standard 8**
Philadelphia's health care departments, managed care organization, and provider organizations, with input from people in recovery, family members and community stakeholders, should develop, implement, and promote a written strategic plan that outlines recovery-oriented, person-first goals, policies, operational plans, and management accountability/oversight mechanisms to provide person-first, and linguistically appropriate services that are recovery-oriented.

**Standard 9**
Philadelphia's health care departments, managed care organization, and provider organizations should conduct initial and ongoing organizational self-assessments of recovery-oriented, person-first related activities and are encouraged to integrate person-first recovery management skills, and linguistic competence-related measures into their internal audits, performance improvement programs, satisfaction assessments performed with persons being served, and outcomes-based evaluations. People in recovery, family members and community stakeholders should be surveyed periodically to ensure fidelity to their quality improvement goals.

**Standard 10**
Philadelphia's health care departments, managed care organization, and provider organizations should ensure that identifying data on the individual person who is receiving services such as race, ethnicity, religion and spirituality, sexual orientation, and spoken and written language are collected in health records, integrated into the organization's management information systems, and periodically updated. The data should be used to ensure the integrity of the services offered by providers as noted in these Standards.

**Standard 11**
Philadelphia's health care departments, managed care organization, and provider organizations should maintain a current demographic, cultural, and epidemiological profile of the community as well as a needs assessment to accurately plan for and implement person-first recovery services that respond to the characteristics of the community in which the service is located.

**Standard 12**
Philadelphia's health care departments, managed care organization, and provider organizations should develop participatory, collaborative partnerships with recovery communities including family members and community stakeholders and utilize a variety of formal and informal mechanisms to facilitate the involvement of both the people who come for services and the community at large in designing and implementing services and activities that are recovery-oriented/person-first.

**Standard 13**
Philadelphia's health care departments, managed care organization, and provider organizations should ensure that conflict and grievance resolution processes are

recovery-oriented, person-first and capable of identifying, preventing, and resolving conflicts or complaints by people who come for services. The procedures should be clear, understandable and in the language(s) of the people being served. People in recovery, their family members and community stakeholders should know how to use them.

**Standard 14**

Philadelphia's health care departments, managed care organization, and provider organizations are encouraged to regularly make available to the public information about their progress and successful innovations in implementing recovery-oriented, person-first standards and activities and to provide public notice in their communities about the availability of this information.

**Standard 15**

Philadelphia's health care departments, managed care organization, and provider organizations authorize person-first alternative and complementary recovery support approaches that ensure engagement, retention and satisfaction with services by the people receiving them. Services offered are those that are defined by the community served as comfortable, appropriate and consistent with their values and worldview and are complementary to their natural healing practices. Where relevant, high performance is indicated by an integration of traditional healing practices and recovery approaches with professional models that capture the best of each.

www.ingramcontent.com/pod-product-compliance
Lightning Source LLC
Chambersburg PA
CBHW020510290526
45786CB00002B/541

* 9 781491 828908 *